A RAW DEAL

TRADE AND THE WORLD'S POOR

Written for Christian Aid by Peter Madden

Published by Christian Aid,
PO Box 100, London SE1 7RT

Cover photograph: Christian Aid/Mike Goldwater

Designed by Shape of Things

Printed by Stanley L Hunt (Printers) Ltd, Rushden

ISBN: 0-904379-16-7

Contents

Acknowledgements

A number of people were kind enough to comment on all or parts of the first draft of the book. My thanks to: Ed Mayo, WDM; Professor Reg Green, IDS; Sheila Page, ODI; Dr Hugh Mason, Portsmouth Polytechnic; Richard Adams, Graham Young and Catherine Howe, Traidcraft; Phil Wells, New Consumer; Kim Shillinglaw, the *Observer*; and Rudy de Meyer, NCOS.

A group of Christian Aid supporters from different parts of the country 'test drove' the book. Thanks to the Rev Andrew Davey, Richard Bainbridge, Gwili Lewis and Geraint Rees.

Within Christian Aid, a number of colleagues offered support and advice, particularly Paul Spray, Wendy Tyndale, Kate Phillips, Robert Archer and Clive Robinson. Rosalind Penney worked wonders in editing and making the text more readable. The Rev Michael Taylor made a major contribution to Chapter six, on which Canon Ronald Preston also commented.

These people are not responsible for the content of the book, but they all helped to make it a better read than it otherwise would have been.

Peter Madden 1992

Note: $ refers to US dollars unless otherwise stated. There is a comprehensive glossary of trade terms on page 84.

One world market

"Before you finish eating your breakfast this morning, you've depended on half the world. This is the way our universe is structured... We aren't going to have peace on earth until we recognise this basic fact."
Martin Luther King

Yona Kateera lives in a small village near Bushenyi town in Uganda. He and his family own a small piece of land on which they used to grow coffee. Yona Kateera comments wistfully that some ten years ago he did not need to roam the cities in search of a job, because he could live comfortably on his earnings from coffee beans. Suddenly in 1989 all this changed.

Coffee was introduced in Uganda at the beginning of this century by the British colonial government. The crop became the life-blood of the country's small farmers, and provided over 90 per cent of Uganda's foreign exchange earnings.

In 1989 world coffee prices plummeted, falling by a third in just a week. For countries like Uganda, the impact was catastrophic. For the small-scale farmers, things were especially tough. It was not even worth their while harvesting the beans.

Yona Kateera can no longer send his children to school or pay for medical treatment. While his income has disappeared, the prices of imported goods have doubled. At 53 years of age he has had to sell what little he has to get by.

So many things that many of us take for granted as part of our everyday lives, such as coffee, sugar, cotton or tea, have a long journey behind them, a journey which begins with people in Third World countries and ends with people like us here. These products are part of a chain which stretches across the world and back again.

Just as trade is part of our everyday lives in this way, this is also the case for the people of the Third World, but in a rather different manner. For them it is a question of livelihood rather than lifestyle. The people who produce the products we consume are often poor people, working for a pittance in difficult conditions. We do not see their

3

lives when we buy something. If we did, we might choose to shop differently.

The way that trade policies and systems affect people is seen quite clearly in Christian Aid's work overseas. When the world tin market crashed in 1985 the whole Bolivian economy was thrown into chaos. Christian Aid-supported projects are helping to pick up the pieces, enabling ex-tin miners to rebuild their lives. In the Caribbean, the charity is working with banana farmers whose livelihoods are at risk from decisions taken five thousand miles away in Brussels, which threaten to take away special trading preferences for their produce.

We do not see their lives when we buy something. If we did, we might choose to shop differently

---

The lives of traditional fishing communities in Namibia are threatened by factory fleets from Europe. Subsidised European beef dumped in west Africa is undermining the way of life of nomadic herdsmen in Burkina Faso, by undercutting the beef they produce.

In India and Bangladesh, successful projects to produce cheap and effective medicines may be wiped out because of changes in world trade rules.

Christian Aid works with people all over the world whose lives are made better or worse by the international trading system. These people suffer from: the rock-bottom prices they receive for their produce; the conditions under which they live and work; the power wielded by giant international companies over all aspects of their lives; and their lack of access to rich countries' finance, technology, information and markets.

Father Paul Caspersz, a Jesuit priest with whom Christian Aid works in Sri Lanka, puts it plainly: "There can be no doubt that one of the main factors promoting poverty and all that flows from poverty – under-nutrition, sometimes persistent hunger, unemployment, slums – is unfair and unjust international trade. This means simply that the prices of Third World exports to the First World are low and the prices of its imports from the First World are high ...Why then do the western, industrialised countries prefer aid to trade? This is the question which our northern partners – interested, as much as ourselves,

Trade can happen at a very local level, such as this car boot sale in the UK.

in a just world order – should investigate."

Why trade?
Trade has been part of our lives for thousands of years. It can happen at a very local level, in street markets or car boot sales in this country, or between continents. Exchanging goods, services and money is how we survive and prosper; it forms the basis of our communities and nations.

But if trade is so damaging to Third World countries, why are they involved in it? Would it not be better to withdraw from the system entirely and seek self-sufficiency?

Withdrawing would be like a suburban family in Dorking or Dublin relying only on what they could grow in their back garden. They might have just enough food, but would be unable to produce medicines, fuel and machinery. A country which had no iron ore would be condemned to the Stone Age. Nations would have to rely only on what they could produce themselves. For most this is not a viable option.

Most countries are now part of a world trading market. In the clothing industry, yarn supplied from Indonesia is converted to cloth in India, tailored in Thailand according

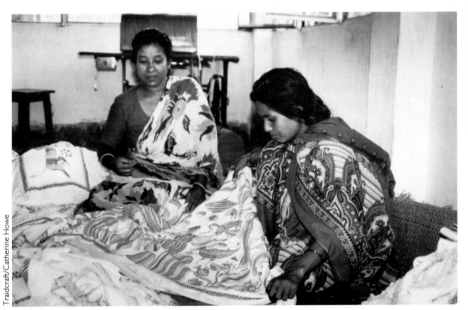

Local women benefit from trade through the Kumudini Welfare Trust in Bangladesh: Tahera and Noorhajen inspect fabrics for export.

to fashions designed in Taiwan and eventually sold in Germany. We are joined together in a giant global system.

Many people argue against becoming part of this system because, they say, the benefits of trade do not reach the poor. In many cases this is true, but to cut off all trade would hurt poor people even more. They usually prefer to have a low wage than no wage, and conditions in the export sector are often better than in other parts of the economy.

The question is not whether to trade or not, but what kind of trade. Trade should benefit the poor, help countries and communities to develop and respect our environment.

Redeeming the trading system
In Bangladesh, one of the poorest countries in the world, the Kumudini Welfare Trust brings the benefits of trade to local women, supported by Christian Aid. The revival of traditional handicrafts and a modern garment factory have provided jobs and enabled the women to learn skills. Exports of these products (to Traidcraft, John Lewis and Liberty in the UK and commercial outlets worldwide) also help to fund health and community development projects all over Bangladesh.

The factory is one of few in Bangladesh which provide women with well-paid work in good conditions, while craft work gives village women a chance to earn money where they need it – in the home. "Embroidery can be done after the household work," explains Tahera, who supervises the scheme. "The money has enabled women to buy cattle and lease land. It is good to earn money at home and their husbands are pleased with the earnings, so there is no tension in the household."

Having extra money has meant that over the years women working for the handicraft centre have become self-reliant and have improved their status in the family. Their children are healthier, because more money is available for food, and family planning has been widely adopted.

Trade should play a positive part in helping communities and countries to develop. However, the biases in the system tend to favour the rich and powerful. Because of historical roots, accidental factors and conscious decisions, the trading system prevents far too many from sharing in the fruits of development.

Giving with one hand . . .

If world trade was organised more fairly and openly, many poor countries would not need so much aid. Instead, through policies such as protectionism, rich countries give with one hand while taking away with the other. According to the 1991 World Bank Development Report: "Unrestricted access to industrial country markets by developing nations would add $55 billion to their export earnings – as much as they receive in aid."

At the moment, aid only accounts for five per cent of all the income of the Third World. Trade, on the other hand, represents more than 80 per cent. In 1985, the year of the Ethiopian famine, the total amount of emergency aid to Africa from all sources was around $3 billion. In the same year, a collapse in world prices for raw materials such as coffee and copper meant that rich countries paid $19 billion less for what they bought from Africa.

This is why Christian Aid believes we must tackle the structures that keep people poor. Of course giving aid is vital, but this only helps a small number of those who need it. For the people of Ghana, a quarter of whom work in the cocoa sector, a few pence more or less on the international market price can have much more impact on their lives. The peoples of Africa, Asia and Latin America want their countries to be able to develop in ways which allow them to stand on their own two feet. They do not look for hand-outs but for just returns, and this means a change in the economic policies of the richer nations.

One world

As well as improving life for millions of people in the Third World, redeeming the trading system can benefit us as well. We live in an increasingly interdependent world in which all the parts need to function and support each other. Environmental catastrophe, mass migration of people and conflict are problems which do not respect borders. Solving these problems means increasing the prosperity of the poor of the world, through policies for fairer trade.

Some people are concerned that competition by Third World producers will put Europeans out of work. But only three per cent of manufactures bought in rich countries are supplied by the Third World. Most jobs are lost in industrialised nations because of new technology rather than cheap imports.

An economically successful Third World should mean

more, not fewer, jobs in rich countries because they would be able to export more. Economist Susan George estimates that, between 1982 and 1988, a total of $171 billion of European exports was lost as a direct result of the economic recession in the Third World. That adds up to between 500,000 and 700,000 jobs a year.

At the moment, aid only accounts for five per cent of all the income of the Third World

---

The new world order

The world trading system is rapidly changing. The Third World is made up of several groups of peoples and countries with very different capabilities and needs, and this is reflected in their economies.

Countries such as South Korea, Taiwan, Hong Kong and Brazil are now challenging the old industrial powers, producing modern, high-tech goods. Meanwhile, most of sub-Saharan Africa is being increasingly pushed to the sidelines. With just under ten per cent of the world's population, it produces less than one per cent of the world's wealth.

Wealthy nations' economies are changing too. Services are replacing industries. Europe is about to form a huge single market and giant international companies are coming to control more and more of our trade.

Many Third World countries and communities are in a position to compete successfully in the world market but they need to be given a level playing field.

Others have been weakened by successive factors since the days of the slave trade. Without compensation they will fall further and further behind. Factors such as power and the extent to which their communities are developed affect the way people can compete in a free market. This is recognised in Europe; disadvantaged regions in the European Community (EC) get subsidies or development grants. The world's poorest and weakest countries also deserve special treatment to compensate them for the structural biases of the system and to allow them eventually to stand on their own feet.

In an increasingly complex world, each country will have different needs and opportunities. Christian Aid is in no position to offer a blueprint for trading success in every case. Specific needs require specific solutions.

However, in the broadest terms Christian Aid believes that success in trade requires two things:

● helpful economic policies within nations

● a favourable international environment

One without the other is unlikely to bring success. There has been much emphasis recently on the failings of Third World countries themselves. Some of this criticism – of corruption for example – was justified. However, many have responded to criticisms and begun to address these problems.

The real problem is the lack of parallel changes in the international system. Only one side of the equation is being addressed.

Time to act
While millions of the world's poor wait for these changes, the situation is getting worse. The World Bank expects prices of raw materials, on which so many rely for survival, to fall even faster in the 1990s than the 1980s, with disastrous consequences for the Third World.

For farmers who rioted in Ivory Coast because of the low cocoa prices; for plantation workers who faced famine in the Philippines, because sugar formerly sold to soft drink factories has been replaced by artificial sweeteners; for the miners in Bolivia now growing coca (for cocaine) as a result of the tin market collapse in 1985; and for Colombian peasants also forced to produce cocaine by rock-bottom coffee prices, it is time for a change.

For the Bangladeshi farmer staring helplessly as the encroaching flood waters lap over the roof of his house; for the ten-year-old girl sitting listlessly in the Sudanese refugee camp, exhausted after a month-long walk from famine-torn Ethiopia; for the doctor in Peru, her hospital filled with cholera patients as the disease rages through her country, reaching epidemic proportions for the first time this century, it is also time for a change.

For the millions of other people who never grab the headlines, but for whom grinding poverty and injustice are a day to day reality, it is time for a change.

CHAPTER TWO

Growing pains

"Whosoever commands the trade of the world commands the riches of the world and hence the world itself."
Sir Walter Raleigh

Like thousands of other Haitians, Lova Constant works on a sugar plantation in the Dominican Republic in the Caribbean. He came from Haiti in 1984, when his country's dictator received millions of dollars a year to supply workers for the neighbouring country's cane fields. "It was even worse then than it is now," says Constant.

It is difficult to imagine harsher conditions. The workers are called 'congos' after their ancestors who arrived in slave ships from the Congo. They live in dirt floored huts made of sticks and mud, roofed with banana leaves. Most sleep on the bare floor wrapped in rags. There is no electricity; light comes from smoky lamps made from tin cans with twisted rags for wicks. One hand pump supplies drinking water for 800 people. They are luckier than many other camps, where drinking water comes from irrigation ditches polluted with pesticides and sewage. Plantation workers are paid about 90p for each tonne of sugar cane cut.

On a good day a cutter can harvest two tonnes. Out of that he has to pay a bribe to the driver of the ox cart, who hauls the cane to the scales, and rent to the company for the 'house' he lives in. "Who knows if the scales are accurate? The scale-men often short weigh us on purpose," says Luis Shaul, leader of the Barahona Cane Cutters' Union.

"All the land belongs to the sugar company, but they will not let us plant anything to eat. During the harvest things aren't so bad, but in the off-season, a person is lucky to work two days a week. If we could plant a few vegetables it would make a big difference."

The plantation workers' story began in 1492 when Columbus sailed in search of a new trade route to the East but landed instead in what we now call the Caribbean.

Christian Aid/Larry Boyd

A Haitian cane cutter shows his meagre earnings.

He established sugar cane on the island of Hispaniola (today Haiti and the Dominican Republic). Like the rest of the Caribbean, the island was cleared, not only of trees but also of people. Once the indigenous people had been wiped out, men and women were brought from Africa as slaves, in order to supply Europe with tropical products.

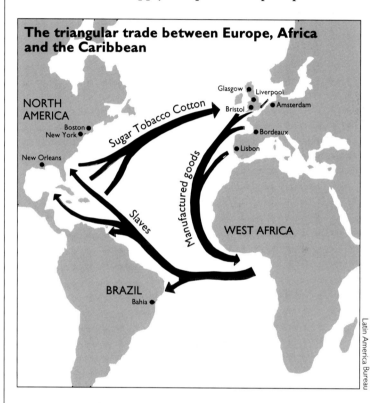

The triangular trade between Europe, Africa and the Caribbean

Latin America Bureau

In the course of three centuries, slavers abducted an estimated five million Africans and sold those who survived the journey in the Caribbean colonies. In the 'triangular trade', ships left ports such as Liverpool or Bristol for Africa, to exchange manufactured goods for slaves. The ships then sailed on to the Caribbean. Sometimes more than half of the consignment died during the voyage and were tossed overboard. The remainder were exchanged for tropical products, such as sugar, for Europe. The early prosperity of cities such as Bristol and Liverpool was built on such trade. Since then the global sugar market has enriched a few but impoverished many.

Commodity dependence

Sugar was just one of the raw materials which spurred European powers to colonise most of the countries now known as the Third World. In return for supplying their imperial masters with this and other raw materials – such as rubber, gold, coffee and tea – countries imported all their manufactured or finished goods from them.

Today empire and slavery have largely disappeared, but many of the basic elements of this system remain, except that now the rich countries are competing with the poor in their own raw materials, or what are called commodities. European beet sugar is taking the place of Third World cane sugar, for example.

Some Third World countries have moved successfully into manufacturing, but this has been concentrated amongst a relatively small number. Seven developing countries account for 70 per cent of manufactured exports from the Third World to industrialised nations.

Most of the poorest Third World countries, particularly in Africa, are still exporters of raw materials and importers of manufactured goods. They lack the skills, infrastructure, technology and finance to produce anything else.

Increasingly these countries also need to export in order to import food for their populations and to pay off debts. Those classified by the United Nations (UN) as 'Least Developed Countries' (LDCs) – such as Haiti, Bolivia and much of sub-Saharan Africa – still rely on commodities for around three quarters of their export earnings – the same proportion as in 1966. Political independence from colonial powers has not meant economic independence.

This reliance means people living in Third World countries are at the mercy of factors outside their control, such as the weather or changes in the trading policies of rich, industrialised nations.

In October 1985 the world price of tin suddenly fell by half – from £8,000 to £4,000 a tonne. What had happened was that the tin producers' attempts to keep a reasonable price suddenly collapsed, unable to counter the mounting pressure of falling demand and increasing supply. Bolivia's entire economy was reliant on tin. Thousands were left without work, government revenues were halved and a proud tradition of trade union protection of workers' rights was destroyed. Overnight, Bolivia became the second poorest country in the Western hemisphere.

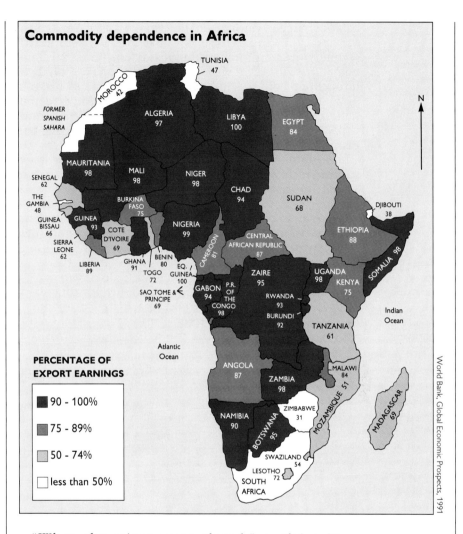

Commodity dependence in Africa

TUNISIA 47

MOROCCO 42

FORMER SPANISH SAHARA

ALGERIA 97

LIBYA 100

EGYPT 84

N

MAURITANIA 98

SENEGAL 62

MALI 98

NIGER 98

CHAD 94

SUDAN 68

DJIBOUTI 38

THE GAMBIA 48

BURKINA FASO 75

GUINEA BISSAU 66

GUINEA 93

COTE D'IVOIRE 69

NIGERIA 99

CENTRAL AFRICAN REPUBLIC 87

ETHIOPIA 88

SIERRA LEONE 62

LIBERIA 89

GHANA 91

BENIN 80

TOGO 72

EQ. GUINEA 100

CAMEROON 81

ZAIRE 95

UGANDA 98

KENYA 75

SOMALIA 98

SAO TOME & PRINCIPE 69

GABON 94

P.R. OF THE CONGO 98

RWANDA 93

BURUNDI 92

TANZANIA 61

Indian Ocean

Atlantic Ocean

ANGOLA 87

MALAWI 84

ZAMBIA 98

MOZAMBIQUE 51

MADAGASCAR 69

ZIMBABWE 31

PERCENTAGE OF EXPORT EARNINGS

NAMIBIA 90

BOTSWANA 95

SWAZILAND 54

LESOTHO 72

SOUTH AFRICA

- ◼ 90 - 100%
- ◼ 75 - 89%
- ◻ 50 - 74%
- ☐ less than 50%

World Bank, Global Economic Prospects, 1991

"When the mines were closed," explains Mery Carmargo, deputy director of OASI, the Church Social Assistance Office, "people were told that there was no work left there. They were told that the sugar and cotton plantations would provide employment."

However, the reality was different. "We know that even a shoeshine boy earns more than we do," says a Bolivian sugar cane cutter, leaning on his machete in the middle of a field. "But what can we do? You have to be a child to shine shoes, and you have to live in the city."

Other tin miners moved into the tropical forest to grow coca or pan for gold, destroying the delicate ecological balance. Others moved to the shanty towns to try to scratch a living. OASI is working with migrant communities to improve living conditions, in partnership with Christian Aid. This is just one of the many projects throughout Bolivia which are helping people to make a new start after the tin collapse. Christian Aid had the same experience in Zambia following the fall in world copper prices. Zambia is 98 per cent reliant on copper for export revenues.

From month to month or year to year, there are huge variations in the prices paid for the commodities on which the poor rely. This has effects at both local and national level. Farm workers who see their income go up and down so dramatically find it as difficult to plan their lives as their governments do to plan the national economies.

A poor return

Commodity producers see very little return for their hard work. Only 12 pence of the cost of a £1.50 jar of coffee, for example, goes to the picker. For this, the second most important commodity in the world, nearly all the roasting, instantising, decaffeinating and packing takes

Who profits? A £1.50 jar of instant coffee

12p Wages

35p Costs of production

18p State*

7p Transport

21p Direct costs of processing**

57p Advertising, overheads and profit**

* COSTA RICA ** U K

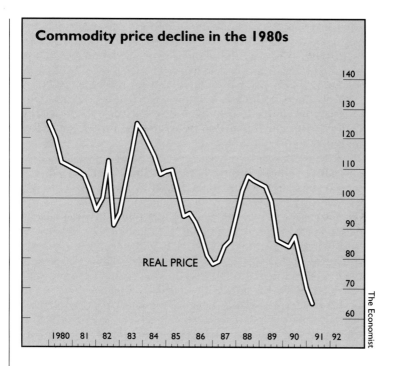

Commodity price decline in the 1980s

REAL PRICE

140
130
120
110
100
90
80
70
60

1980 81 82 83 84 85 86 87 88 89 90 91 92

The Economist

place in rich countries. The story is the same for other commodities: the profitable stages of production such as processing, packaging and marketing are usually controlled by multinational companies and take place in the industrialised nations.

There is also a long-term decline in the price paid for commodities relative to that of other goods. Jeffrey Perreira, the Director of Caritas, the Catholic development agency in Bangladesh, explains: "When we bought a power-tiller 20 years ago, it cost us 1.5 tonnes of raw jute. A similar power-tiller today costs us nine tonnes."

This fall was particularly dramatic during the 1980s, when the value of commodities fell by a third.

As well as harming the poor directly, this loss of earnings has reduced government spending in areas such as social services and reduced the ability to import vital supplies such as medicines, machinery and, increasingly, food.

The cause of the crisis
Third World commodity producers receive such low returns for a number of reasons. One major factor is that there is chronic oversupply in most of the markets.

Unable to produce manufactured goods and desperate for foreign exchange, many Third World countries compete with each other in the same commodities – cocoa for chocolate, for example, is grown in Africa, Asia and Latin America. Even if farmers have the money and skills to shift production, it takes a number of years to re-adjust to changes in demand, for example four years to grow a coffee bush, and much longer to develop new skills and markets.

Another reason for low returns is the collapse of nearly all International Commodity Agreements (ICAs). These were established to maintain prices in the 1970s, the era of 'commodity power'. With Third World countries working together to get higher prices, and worries about shortages of natural resources, it was believed that they held a trump card in negotiations with rich countries. But the inflexibility of ICAs, the emerging debt crisis and desperate competition between the countries involved have led to the breakdown of virtually all ICAs.

The debt crisis made things even worse. Many Third World countries borrowed heavily in the 1970s, encouraged to do so by large commercial banks in Europe, the United States and Japan. The banks were keen

Running faster to stand still: volume of exports and terms of trade

Volume of exports

Terms of trade

Index: 1965 = 100

World Bank 1991

to lend out the huge amounts of money deposited with them by the oil-producing countries of OPEC – the spoils of quadrupling the price of oil. Unfortunately commodity prices fell at the same time as interest rates on the loans rose, leaving Third World countries with too little income from exports to pay off their debts. They were then desperate to earn foreign exchange and so exported more and more, pushing prices lower and lower. They were running faster to stand still. Thailand increased its rubber exports by a third in 1985, but its total earnings fell by eight per cent because of a drop in the world price.

Commodity prices fell at the same time as interest rates on the loans rose, leaving Third World countries with too little income from exports to pay off their debts

---

The International Monetary Fund (IMF) and the World Bank exacerbated the situation by refusing to allow debtor countries access to loans unless they agreed to increase their exports. This policy (known as 'structural adjustment') encouraged Third World countries to produce more of the same commodities for shrinking, recession-hit markets.

Until 1984, prices for palm oil, unlike most other commodities, remained fairly stable. This led a number of countries in sub-Saharan Africa to follow World Bank advice and invest heavily in palm oil production. At the same time, however, high world prices and the collapse of other commodity markets led traditional suppliers in Asia to step up their own investment. The inevitable result was a slump in 1985-6 during which prices fell to their lowest real terms since the 1930s.

Despite the fact that there was no prospect of even a medium term recovery, the World Bank then committed over $2 billion to promoting Indonesian palm production. The EC also supported a massive expansion of palm oil production in Ghana, in one of its largest aid projects in sub-Saharan Africa. The World Bank has now admitted its folly in this case, but the overall policy of promoting commodity exports remains.

The rich countries, rather than the poor, have benefited from such policies. The commodity price collapse played a major part in conquering inflation in such countries by drastically cutting the price of production. Today wealthy nations benefit to the tune of one per cent of Gross Domestic Product (GDP) from lower raw material costs. At the same time they cannot even reach the UN minimum target of 0.7 per cent of Gross National Product (GNP) in aid to Third World countries.

Changes in the First World

The future for commodity producers remains bleak. Even if they can work together to ensure higher prices, there are a number of negative trends in the rich, industrialised world which poorer countries are powerless to influence.

Rich or First World countries have developed substitutes for many of the commodities on which the Third World relies.

Artificial rubber has replaced the natural variety in many uses, synthetics such as nylon have been substituted for cotton. Instead of using copper, developed countries are increasingly using fibre optics (made from glass) for telephone wires or plastic pipes for plumbing. Developments in 'biotechnology', whereby scientists can manipulate animals and plants by changing and transferring genes, make rich countries less dependent on crops from poorer countries.

A product called Thaumautin is also being developed which is 3,000 times as sweet as sugar

---

Cane sugar from the Third World is under threat from substitutes in this way. Corn syrup, extracted from maize, now provides 60 per cent of the US sweetener market. When this product first began to displace sugar, the US slashed its sugar imports. This led to a famine in 1985 on the fertile Philippine island of Negros, where a quarter of a million people were left without work. A product called Thaumautin is also being developed which is 3,000 times as sweet as sugar. It cannot be long before this is produced in factories in rich countries.

Another trend is that industrialised countries' economies are changing, reducing the amount of commodities needed. Services are now more important than manufactures, and even within industry, the old 'smoke stack' industries are being replaced by 'sunrise' ones such as electronics, which require smaller quantities of raw materials.

Improved design has also led to reduced demand for raw materials. To save on fuel cars are now lighter, made with less metal and more plastic. Environmental concern means that recycling is on the increase. These trends,while not bad in themselves, have serious

---

The World Bank expects that, in the year 2000, the commodity price index will still be barely half the 1950 level

---

consequences for people living in Third World countries.

Changes in eastern Europe and in some of the more industrialised developing countries such as South Korea, may provide new markets for the Third World. But this will take time and is unlikely to outweigh the losses.

Classical economic theory argues that countries should produce what they can most cheaply and trade these products for other goods. Modern common sense suggests that it would be suicidal for Third World countries to decide that their future lies with commodities. They may be able to produce them cheaply, but if the price is declining and substitutes are threatening, if there is over-production and rich countries now do most of their trading with each other, continuing to rely on commodities appears foolhardy. The World Bank expects that, in the year 2000, the commodity price index will still be barely half the 1950 level.

A better deal

People in poor countries which rely on commodities can have a better deal – by stabilising prices, ensuring a better return and moving away from commodity dependence.

One way is to do more of the processing and marketing of the raw materials they produce. Christian Aid and the alternative trading organisation, Twin Trading, support UCOBAM, a fruit and vegetable co-operative in Burkina Faso, in processing and marketing their produce in order to gain added value.

Instead of others reaping the profits, or bumper harvests going to waste because of lack of processing, marketing or transport facilities, a small factory is now producing exotic jams and preserves for export to west Africa and Europe. Delicious mango preserve is now available in the

UK through Twin Trading.

Alternatively, producers can move sideways into producing a wider range of products for domestic markets and try for greater regional or local trade. Ultimately, for any country, some kind of manufacturing base is desirable.

These ways of developing a more balanced and stable economy, spreading risks and increasing participation and flexibility are known as 'diversification'.

Ultimately, for any country, some kind of manufacturing base is desirable

In the village of Loumbila in Burkina Faso, a group supported by Christian Aid, Wend Yam Federation, has helped local people to diversify. Instead of depending on their income from casual labour or traditional commodities, they now produce a steady income selling beans, tomatoes, cabbages, aubergines, potatoes and carrots. The village men use machetes and spades to clear the land of tall bush grass. Men and women work together on sowing, weeding and harvesting, the women carrying their babies in slings on their backs as they work.

"During the dry season, before we had this farm our young people had to go to the towns to earn extra income," says Alassane Ilboudo, Secretary of the Village Committee. "That's why when you pass through a lot of villages all you see are old men and old women – everyone else has left."

Now, with the help of Christian Aid, they have employment and a new source of income. It takes just 45 days to grow a single crop of beans from seed. In the second year, export of the crop raised £2,500 allowing them to pay off loans and still have a sizeable profit.

The beans are sold to Europe, mainly France, and the revenue has helped to fund terracing and tree planting to protect the local environment.

The people of Loumbila village are producing a new product for foreign markets. This is another way in which poor producers can reduce dependence on a traditional commodity.

Snakes and ladders
Moving away from commodity dependence is, however,

Christian Aid/Martin Cottingham

Growing seedlings in Burkina Faso.

23

extremely difficult. It requires skills, technology, knowledge of markets, and money. These are in short supply in communities in the Third World and often in the hands of large companies operating in several countries, called 'transnational corporations' (TNCs).

And, as the Director of Caritas in Bangladesh explains, the trade policies of the rich, industrialised countries often make it even more difficult.

"Each time we seem to succeed in exporting, something in the developed world seems to take it away. Right now we are doing marvellously in garments, giving women tremendous power. But all could be wiped out in seconds either by quotas or automation in the North – I have seen a garment factory in Chicago where nine people do the work 180 did before."

Rich countries' governments penalise the entry of processed goods from the Third World, in order to protect their industries from competition. While raw materials may be allowed in duty free, processed products – such as chocolate from cocoa and furniture

EC tariffs on processed commodities

	Av. tariff rate %
Raw coffee	9.0
Roasted, ground coffee	6.5
Coffee extracts, preparations	18.0
Cocoa beans	3.0
Cocoa butter	12.0
Cocoa paste	15.0
Cocoa powder and chocolate	16.0
Tropical fruit, fresh, dried	8.0
Preserved tropical fruit	11.3
Prepared tropical fruit and juices	23.6

> **The Multi Fibre Arrangement (MFA)**
>
> Under the MFA, industrialised countries place quotas on imports of textiles and clothing from Third World countries. Instituted in 1974 as a 'temporary' measure to control such imports, 18 years later it is still discriminating against the poor. Nor has it protected jobs in the rich countries – new technology has seen to that.
>
> The IMF estimates that abolition of the MFA would raise restricted countries' exports into the industrialised nations of the Organisation for Economic Co-operation and Development (OECD) by 82 per cent for textiles and 93 per cent for clothing. This would mean a 40 per cent increase in textile and clothing employment in MFA-restricted countries. The poorest countries would particularly benefit from the abolition of the MFA.

from timber – face significantly higher barriers. The greater the degree of processing, the higher the tariff or tax. The EC duty on cocoa beans, for example, is three per cent, on cocoa butter 12 per cent and on cocoa paste 15 per cent. This policy helps maintain the Third World as 'hewers of wood and drawers of water'.

Basic industrial goods which Third World countries can most easily make, such as clothing, also face barriers which discriminate against them. The Multi Fibre Arrangement (MFA – see box above) which restricts textile exports from poor countries, but not from rich ones, is a particularly harmful case. Similar problems are faced for shoes, toys and leather products. Other invisible barriers such as transport, packaging, marketing and information also play their part.

A better future?

Many commodity exporters face a very difficult future. With prices fluctuating so wildly and declining over time, debt repayments, lack of investment and changes in rich countries' economies and trading patterns, it is extremely hard for the poor to gain more profit from trade.

They need a fairer price for their commodities, one that more fully reflects the social and environmental costs of production.

They also deserve special treatment to escape dependence. Otherwise they will remain condemned by a system not of their own making.

CHAPTER THREE

How the Third World is taken to market

"The market is a good servant, although quite clearly a bad master."
Simba Makoni, Executive Secretary of Southern African Development
Co-ordination Conference (SADCC)

"Why should we bother to produce if neighbouring countries do it better and cheaper?" asks the Bolivian Minister of Planning. Should a poor Third World country open up to cheap or subsidised foreign imports in the name of economic efficiency?

High up on the Bolivian 'altiplano', a barren, almost treeless region, some of the poorest people in Latin America eke out a living. For these people, almost all indigenous Indians, removing barriers to foreign imports has been disastrous. "Opening up the country meant the closure of more than 150 factories in 1987 alone. Things have become worse and worse for the small rural producer whose traditional markets have been wiped out," explains Javier Guillaumet, Director of the Church Office for Social Assistance in Bolivia.

"Instead Bolivians now buy agricultural products from Chile, Brazil or Argentina in their local market. More than three and a half million peasants have lost the market for their products. They are getting poorer and poorer every day and they now run the risk of having their land repossessed by the State which will then sell it to private investors."

Past errors

Ironically, many people in the Third World suffered in the past because their countries were too protective of their own industries and over-emphasised self-sufficiency. Many poor countries tried to save on imports by producing more at home only to find that they still had to import the means to produce. Industrialisation which relied heavily on machinery and finance, which these countries did not have, rather than labour, which they had in abundance, brought little employment and at the same time denied resources to the agricultural sector.

In some countries, excessive government interference led to large bureaucracies and inefficiency, and state and private monopolies bred corruption and waste. Blanket and heavy-handed protection often produced inefficient companies supplying inferior products.

As Bolivia's example shows, however, the answer to these past mistakes clearly does not lie in simply opening up markets and deregulating (a package generally called neo-liberalism). Nevertheless, this is what countries in the Third World have been pressed into doing throughout the 1980s by the IMF and World Bank in the name of efficiency. While efficiency is important, a pragmatic approach which puts people first, not last, will be much more successful.

Markets and people

In 1983 Ghana signed an agreement with the IMF whereby, in return for new loans the government agreed to launch Africa's first structural adjustment programme, cutting public spending and liberalising trade and exchange controls.

Ghana became the IMF's star pupil, achieving an average growth rate of five per cent in the late 1980s. But more than 100,000 state employees lost their jobs through cuts, and the cost of living rose sharply while wage settlements fell behind food price increases.

"People are living on borrowed money and selling their possessions at giveaway prices"

When a new daily minimum wage of 218 cedis (about 30p) was announced in 1990, the Trades Union Congress calculated that an average family needed C2,000 a day for food alone. "In rural areas," says James Tia of the Churches Commission for Participation in Development, "people are living on borrowed money and selling their possessions at giveaway prices."

Opening the economy led to a surge in second-hand clothing imports, forcing closures in Ghana's textile and clothing industries. Local rice has accumulated in silos, unable to compete against imported rice, subsidised by foreign governments. Levels of malnutrition are rising and

27

Christian Aid/Chris Steele-Perkins

Eking out a living on the Bolivian altiplano.

education is going backwards: while just over half of the 25-34 year age group is illiterate, the figure is 89 per cent for 9-14 year olds.

"Structural adjustment has only benefited the well-to-do while the poor have become poorer," says Joseph Annan, Director of the Methodist Church's Bureau of Social Responsibility in Ghana. "My concern is that whatever gains we have made should be spread among the whole population."

Unfettered markets hurt both people and the planet. Even if letting them work freely brings success in economic terms the social cost can be great. Bishop Abastoflor of Bolivia has criticised the over-emphasis on markets, saying that "people must come before the model, because we cannot subordinate the destiny of the people to theories that are always imperfect."

What markets can and cannot do

Markets are an efficient way of allowing supply to respond effectively to demand. They cannot, however, do everything. Markets discriminate systematically against the poor and weak, both on a national and international level. They can function effectively, however, if certain conditions are met. Third World governments will have to intervene: to deal with concentrations of market power, where a company or group of companies distort a market for their own ends; to provide public infrastructure such as transport or energy systems; and to ensure poor people's needs are met even when they do not have enough money to buy what they need.

They also have to act to protect new industries (as all successful developed and developing countries have done in the past) which will otherwise be crushed by international competition before they get going.

Many poor countries do not have the necessary conditions for markets to work effectively. These must be put in place before the economy is opened up, otherwise what little people have will disappear.

The myth of the market

When those countries who are being encouraged today to 'let markets work' find that this policy does not succeed it is assumed that it is not the theory that is at fault, but the rigour with which it is applied. In fact 'free trade' is something of a myth: the economic success of present rich countries has little to do with it.

While rich countries are telling poor ones to open up their markets, they are becoming more protectionist themselves

After the Second World War, the Allies did not dare impose a programme of 'leaving it to the market' on war-torn Europe, even though its situation was better than that of many eastern European and Third World countries today. The post-War adjustment and liberalisation programmes were extremely cautious and assisted for four years by around $200 billion a year (at today's prices) of US aid, of which three quarters were straight grants. It was not until 1953 that Germany abandoned direct controls on incomes and prices of capital goods and it took France until 1958. Yet today developing countries and eastern Europe are expected to do the same in a matter of months.

The most quoted examples of market-led success in the Third World are the so-called 'newly industrialising countries' (NICs) – South Korea, Singapore, Taiwan and Hong Kong – which have enjoyed spectacular growth of exports and incomes from the 1960s onwards. Yet all the recent studies have shown that these countries' governments actively intervened with industrial policies, strategic protection and targeted export promotion to set a framework for the market, and to propel these economies to where they are today.

Besides protectionism and government intervention, the other major factor that brought trading success to the countries of south east Asia was access to rich countries' markets. This is also being denied to the Third World.

One rule for the rich?

While rich countries are telling poor ones to open up their markets, they are becoming more protectionist themselves. The *Financial Times* (8/11/91) described how, "As many developing countries cut tariffs, the developed world imposes more trade restraints ... Protectionism is if anything growing."

Twenty of the 24 wealthy industrialised nations which make up the Organisation for Economic Co-operation and Development (OECD) are, on balance, more protectionist now than they were ten years ago. While the post-War trend has been to reduce overt protectionism, the rich countries have found a host of other ways to keep out Third World imports.

These are known as 'non-tariff barriers' (NTBs), and currently affect almost 30 per cent of exports from the Third World to the industrialised countries. By contrast, only ten per cent of exports from other rich countries are affected in this way. Barriers are particularly high on the goods that are most important to poor countries.

This protectionism hits such countries hard. The World Bank estimates that the costs exceed official aid from industrial nations, while the Third World countries in the United Nations Conference on Trade and Development (UNCTAD – see box page 40) put the figure at twice as high as official aid. In the textile and clothing sector alone losses of $11 billion and $31 billion have been calculated by the World Bank and UNCTAD respectively.

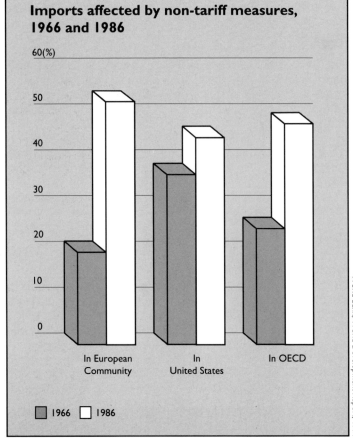

Imports affected by non-tariff measures, 1966 and 1986

60(%)

50

40

30

20

10

0

In European Community In United States In OECD

■ 1966 □ 1986

World Bank, World Development Report, 1991

It is clear that without access to markets, poor countries will remain reliant on aid.

Unilateral disarmament

The General Agreement on Tariffs and Trade (GATT – see box overleaf) lists a whole host of measures taken by poor countries to open up their markets which have not been reciprocated by the rich ones.

The Third World, which is in a much weaker position, should not be forced to open up its markets before the rich countries open theirs. Poor countries need to liberalise on a selective basis with protection for the most vulnerable sectors.

When they have strong and advanced economic institutions, markets that work and competitive industries, this is the time to open up. But this needs to

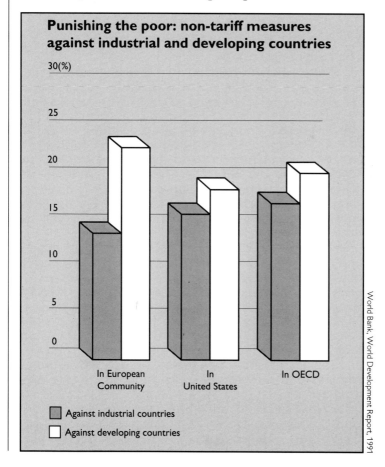

Punishing the poor: non-tariff measures against industrial and developing countries

World Bank, World Development Report, 1991

The General Agreement on Tariffs and Trade (GATT)

The GATT was founded in 1948 to negotiate rules and standards for conducting international trade. The original intention had been to set up an International Trading Organisation (ITO) as an agency of the UN, but the US Congress rejected it and instead the more modest GATT was created.

The basic principle of the GATT is the idea of Most Favoured Nation – that every signatory has to offer the same trading terms to all other signatories as it does to its most favoured trading partner. This was to prevent a return to the dog-eat-dog protectionism of the 1930s.

Successive rounds of GATT have liberalised world trade, but the industrial countries have found more and more ways to take protectionist measures outside its rules.

---

happen gradually, allowing governments to pursue an active industrial policy – as did Japan, Germany and the NICs of south east Asia.

The case of agriculture

As *Hungry Farmers*, an earlier Christian Aid book, showed, agriculture is one area where double standards are particularly damaging. Wealthy companies and countries often dump cheap or subsidised food on the world market. This destroys the livelihood of Third World farmers. It also allows poor countries' governments to neglect their agricultural sector (the largest and poorest part of the Third World) because the politically more influential urban population can be given access to cheap food. Such farmers deserve protection and Third World governments have an obligation to make sure all their people are fed.

The EC and the US have boosted their own agricultural production through excluding foreign foods and through incentives. Their produce now dominates the world market. They have funded wasteful and environmentally damaging programmes, benefiting rich farmers and harming poor farmers. But when poor countries, whose farmers make up a much larger part of the population and who face the day to day reality of starvation, try to use protectionism to raise food production and provide rural employment, they face penalties imposed by the rich nations.

The dumping of subsidised agricultural products by the EC is ruining the livelihood of many farmers in Africa, frustrating regional trade and threatening the environment.

In west Africa Christian Aid supports farmers in the dry lands of northern Burkina Faso, who rely on cattle rearing for their livelihood. This is particularly suited to the fragile ecology of this drought-prone area and provides a valuable source of income and security.

The farmers used to sell beef to neighbouring countries such as Senegal and Ivory Coast. The EC has wiped out their economic base by dumping frozen beef, subsidised by US$2 – $4 a kilo, on west African markets.

Jean Marie Kabore, who lives in Oudalan, describes the impact: "Everything here relies on the income from selling animals. The family budget, cultural life, health – you've just got to sell animals to honour commitments and take care of the family, and your wife and children's health. And if the animals don't sell, or are sold at a derisory price, it's obvious that a man can't keep his family in health.

"Since the international dumping started we are no longer able to sell our animals. To stop it, all we can do at the moment is rely on making foreign opinion more aware of what this is doing to us."

The agricultural trade policies of the rich countries benefit few and harm many. Less agricultural protectionism by rich countries could bring significant trading benefits to the poor ones, and it would also benefit consumers here. A study by the Trade Policy Research Centre says that removing such protection and subsidies would mean an annual gain of $1500 for each non-farm household in the EC.

Helping markets to work

In the arena of world trade there is not a level playing field. Some groups come to market with much greater advantages and are likely to do better. This would suggest the need for compensatory mechanisms to even things out. Markets require a regulatory system in order to work for the benefit of all.

A mixture of compensation and regulation is needed. It would entail different treatment for rich and poor countries, and would have to have a strong institutional base, so that the powerful do not abuse their power.

Trade, power and the GATT

Throughout the 1980s, rich countries have consistently found ways to abuse their position in trade agreements. Non-tariff barriers, the MFA and agricultural subsidies are prime examples.

Christian Aid/Margaret Murray

Traditional animal husbandry in Burkina Faso is under threat because of European trading policies.

There are international rules laid down by the GATT, yet it is almost impossible to enforce these on economic superpowers like the US and EC. They can back out of GATT principles by taking unilateral and bilateral measures, and ignoring unfavourable verdicts on their trade practices.

Through Section 301 of its Trade Act, the US has taken it upon itself to be judge and jury, as well as prosecutor, in deciding what constitutes unfair competition. If another country is being too successful in exporting, the US can threaten severe retaliation unless the country restrains itself. This process is of course open to abuse by domestic manufacturing lobbies calling for protection.

There are other reasons too why it is questionable whether the GATT in its present form is the body to provide the firm regulation which world trade needs.

The GATT is biased towards the richer nations, both in the issues it covers and the negotiating process. Decision-making is hidden and national parliaments are presented with a fait accompli. Corporate business interests are taken into consideration because of their strong lobbying position. Organisations representing other areas of society such as consumer, environmental or Third World interests have very little access. Consequently, the social and environmental impacts of GATT agreements receive little attention, even though these may be severe.

There are international rules laid down by the GATT, yet it is almost impossible to enforce these on economic superpowers like the US and EC

The GATT also has a very narrow focus. The fact that the world economy is increasingly interdependent, with strong interlinkages between trade, technology, investment and services, means that it no longer makes sense to treat 'trade' in isolation. Nor does GATT address the growing power of major international companies in world trade.

A new international trading organisation?
There is widespread agreement that something should replace or enhance the GATT after the current round of negotiations. The question is, what?

An open, multilateral trading organisation needs to fulfil certain criteria. Human and environmental objectives should be at the heart of trade policy, not an afterthought. There should be positive mechanisms to promote Third World trade in a way that can be sustained. The institution must be participative, allowing a voice for all countries, and have the power to enforce its regulations.

The financial and monetary policies of rich countries, such as high interest rates, hardly take into account the impact on poor countries

Co-ordination is also important. As we have seen, the IMF and World Bank expect Third World countries to increase their export earnings, but at the same time the GATT cannot prevent the growth of protectionism in the important markets in the rich countries. In the GATT negotiations, poor countries are pressed to make trade concessions, but no credit is given for the liberalisation undertaken under structural adjustment programmes. The financial and monetary policies of rich countries, such as high interest rates, hardly take into account the impact on poor countries.

The need for improved co-ordination and regulation in world trade has led many to call for a new ITO. An ITO was nearly formed after World War Two as the third part of a system of international economic co-ordination – the other two parts being the IMF and World Bank – but it died an early death. Some have argued that the international system cannot balance on two legs alone, but needs this third leg firmly in place. There is now widespread support for a new initiative in this area, an organisation that would subsume the GATT and UNCTAD and be able to regulate world trade.

The EC has put a more modest proposal on the table for a Multilateral Trade Organisation to administer the GATT agreements, but its structure remains undecided. It is to be hoped that it will prove more transparent, equitable and democratic than the GATT and have the power to regulate rich countries and rich companies. It needs to give far more attention to the developmental and environmental impact of trade and the interlinkages in the world system.

The rise and fall of UNCTAD

The United Nations Conference on Trade and Development was established in 1964 at the behest of Third World countries who did not feel that the GATT addressed their needs adequately.

UNCTAD has a strong Third World presence and has tended to look at trade in a wider, developmental framework. However, it never received the necessary political support from the major trading nations, and, like many other UN agencies where the poor countries have some influence, has been pushed to the sidelines.

Governments in Europe have become increasingly vocal about the need for Third World countries to become democratic. But why should Europe's concern stop at national boundaries? Salim Salim, the Secretary General of the Organisation of African Unity, puts the case starkly. "While Africa must democratise, our efforts will be hamstrung by the non-democratic international system in which we operate. Multipartyism will not change the price of coffee, cotton, sisal or copper. Africa is not consulted on how the world is run, or worse still on the prices of her commodities. Logically I would have thought that an argument for democratisation of African societies would have been linked to the democratisation of the international system."

What is certain is that international trade needs a rule-based system which gives special treatment to the poor as well as the rich. This does not mean that markets do not have an important role to play, rather that they will be helped to function more efficiently in some areas by being more constrained in others. Managed markets in a multilateral system should be the way forward.

CHAPTER FOUR

Business as usual?

"What if the man from Del Monte says no?"
Ibarra Malonzo, President of the National Federation of Labour,
the Philippines

Although the tendency is to think of world trade as between countries, with independent buyers and sellers, in fact most of it takes place between companies. Since the Second World War, a few giant companies operating in several countries, known as transnational corporations (TNCs), have come to dominate the world market.

TNCs are among the most powerful economic institutions in the world. Companies such as Nestlé, Hitachi and Unilever have turnovers of around £20 billion a year, bigger than the value of the exports of all but five Third World countries. The combined turnover of the top 200 corporations is the equivalent of a third of the world's GDP.

In the areas they dominate, TNCs usually control the whole production chain from start to finish. For example, Unilever and its subsidiaries, Lipton and Brooke Bond, control at least 30 per cent of world tea production, trade and processing.

Their sheer size and power mean that TNCs have the ability to do a great deal of good, or a great deal of harm. They can decide the fate of whole communities, even countries, and, unlike governments, there is no system of accountability.

Sierra Leone: priced into poverty

Lying on the tip of tropical west Africa, Sierra Leone enjoys a number of natural advantages: fertile soil, a small population and coastal waters teeming with fish. It also has rich deposits of bauxite (for aluminium), rutile (for titanium), and diamonds.

Yet, according to the United Nations Development Programme, Sierra Leone now has the worst standard of living in the world. Seventy per cent of its people live in absolute poverty and, at 42 years, average life expectancy is lower than that of any other country.

It is the story of an increasing decline into poverty,

which Sierra Leone was unable to use its mineral wealth to eliminate. Like many other Third World countries, it lacked the finance, technical expertise and know-how to exploit its resources. Instead it invited in foreign TNCs.

Its bauxite is mined by Sieromco, a wholly-owned subsidiary of the Swiss aluminium giant, Alusuisse. The company turns over more than $25 million a year, but the ordinary daily wage they pay labourers is 60p with a bag of rice once a month.

The government of neighbouring Guinea makes around $24 a tonne in revenue from bauxite exports. The government of Sierra Leone is lucky to see one tenth of that.

Alusuisse, the parent company, buys all of Sieromco's bauxite at a fixed price which has nothing to do with market forces. In 1989 Alusuisse paid Sieromco around $15 per tonne for Sierra Leonian bauxite. By the time it had reached Germany, the same bauxite had miraculously more than doubled in value. Alusuisse was paid $33.45 a tonne for it. Even given costs such as transport and insurance, this is still a huge profit.

This process, known as transfer pricing, is one of the many ways major international companies can use 'free trade' for their own ends. As an estimated 40 per cent of world trade takes place within companies, there is plenty of room for creative accounting. It is estimated that transfer pricing by Alusuisse has cost Sierra Leone over $100 million since 1980.

With the help of the UN, the Sierra Leonian government recently signed a new agreement with the other major mining company operating in the country, Sierra Rutile Ltd. This, and increased production, have raised government income dramatically and the company now contributes up to ten times as much as it used to.

Sierra Leone's problems are an example of those faced by Third World countries. They need TNCs, but often get a bad deal.

Technology

To be able to sell a product in the world market, people or companies in the Third World need to be able to produce it cheaply, at an expected quality, and in accordance with the changing demands of consumers – and the moneyed consumers are in rich, industrialised countries.

Knowledge of technology and markets is in the hands of TNCs. These companies continually develop

technology and both create and respond to changing
market demand. Thus the Third World needs access to a
flow of technology and information to remain up-to-date.
But it is in a weak bargaining position. Realising their
competitive advantage, TNCs restrict access to their
knowledge and technology. If the rich nations get their
way in the latest GATT talks, known as the 'Uruguay
Round', international restrictions on patents and
intellectual property are likely to be tightened, giving
TNCs even more power vis-à-vis poor countries. Without
new technology Third World countries will not be able
to produce without damaging the environment or at a
competitive price.

Tackling TNCs – drugs in Bangladesh
The World Health Organisation lists about 250 essential
medicines that should be widely available. Not enough of
these vital medicines are produced within Third World
countries. Instead, major international companies sell
them at inflated prices, making huge profits. At the same
time they promote expensive tonics of little, if any, value
to health.

A group supported by Christian Aid in Bangladesh,
Gonoshasthaya Kendra (the People's Health Centre),
realised it had to shake up the whole drug business if it
was to serve the needs of poor people.

"Drugs are a commodity, just like a shirt or a blouse,"
says Dr Zafrullah Chowdhury, Gonoshasthaya Kendra's
founder. "But with most commodities, such as clothes,
consumers can check for themselves whether the product
is worth the price.

"In the case of drugs there are too many powerful
intermediaries, including doctors and chemists, for most
people to be able to make an informed choice. Drug
producers, like those of any other commodity, take
advantage of this powerlessness."

Gonoshasthaya Kendra set up their own factory to
manufacture these essential medicines and found that
they could produce them – including aspirin and
penicillin – at a cost 35 to 50 per cent less than that of
drugs produced by multinational companies.

At first they came up against fierce opposition from the
companies. Undaunted, Gonoshasthaya Kendra pressured
the Bangladeshi government to change its drugs policy. In
1982 the government passed a new Drugs Law under
which 1,700 drugs described as "harmful or unnecessary"
were banned. The flood of imported useless drugs

43

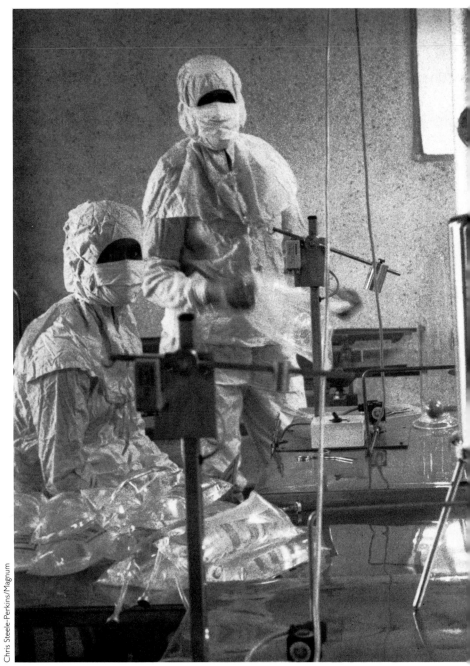

Chris Steele-Perkins/Magnum

The production of cheap, essential medicines in this Christian Aid-funded factory in Bangladesh is under threat from major international companies.

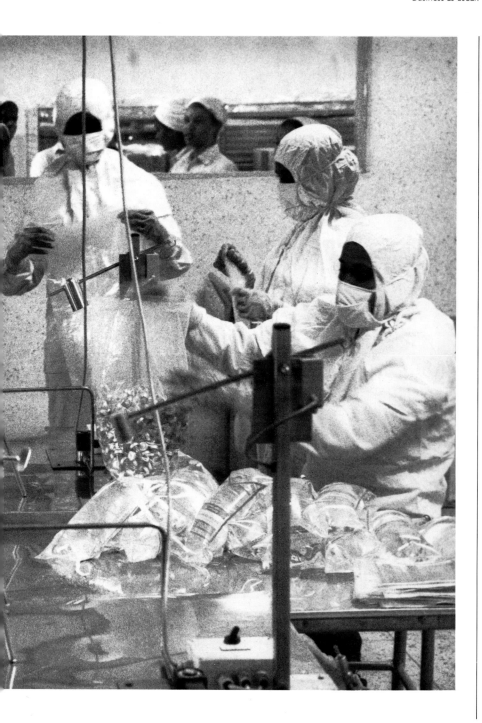

decreased, and more drugs were available at prices the poor could afford. This good work is now under threat as TNCs fight to regain their market.

Because they are transnational, these companies cannot be expected to have a major commitment to the countries they are working in. If they are offered a better deal, they can shift production from one country to another. They can easily play poor countries off against each other.

The profits made by TNCs are not necessarily re-invested in the host country, but sent home to companies or shareholders in rich countries. TNCs do bring jobs and revenues but in return Third World countries forego the chance to plan their own development and, instead, hand over economic control to outside organisations more

Market share of transnational companies in world primary commodity trade

CEREALS 5 COMPANIES		**77%**
BANANAS 3 COMPANIES		**80%**
COCOA 3 COMPANIES		**83%**
TEA 3 COMPANIES		**85%**
TOBACCO 4 COMPANIES		**87%**

With so many commodity producers and so few buyers the price will tend to stay low.

B. Delpeuch

concerned with their own profits.

There is also a concentration of power among TNCs. As a result of mergers and take-overs, an ever smaller number of ever bigger companies are coming to dominate world trade.

The weak bargaining position of Third World countries means that many are falling over each other to see who can offer major international companies the best terms.

Because they are transnational, these companies cannot be expected to have a major commitment to the countries they are working in. They can easily play poor countries off against each other

From foe to friend

The 1980s saw a dramatic change in poor countries' attitude towards TNCs. During the 1970s such companies were a major cause of concern and controversy. Nationalisation and expropriation by Third World countries became the fashion. In 1975 the assets of 83 foreign companies were confiscated. Ten years later this only happened to one.

Why had things changed so radically? The conditions that had attracted major international companies to the Third World were changing. Automation meant that cheap labour was no longer such an attraction. Direct labour costs as a percentage of total production costs in US industry fell from 30 per cent to ten per cent over the past 20 years. Increasing protectionism by rich, industrialised countries also meant that access to markets was an important factor in where companies located.

In addition, a decade of crippling debt repayments and a huge drop in foreign investment meant that Third World governments came to see TNCs as the only source of investment, skills and technology.

Free trade zones

In their desperation to attract foreign companies many Third World countries are now setting up free trade zones. These are havens for foreign investment, complete with government-subsidised electricity and tax concessions. They mean more freedom for business and less for people. Trade unions, strikes and freedom of movement are severely limited or forbidden.

Eighty to 90 per cent of the light-assembly workers in free trade zones are women. Although factory work benefits them by enabling them to earn money and work outside their homes, it has a negative side too. Since women everywhere are paid lower wages than men, they are the obvious choice for major international companies, which go overseas to reduce labour costs.

Women are seen as having "natural patience" and "manual dexterity". A manager of an assembly plant in Taiwan explains: "Young male workers are too restless and impatient to do monotonous work with no career value. If displeased they sabotage the machines and even threaten the foreman. But girls, at most they cry a little."

Since women everywhere are paid lower wages than men, they are the obvious choice for major international companies, which go overseas to reduce labour costs

---

In these Third World export processing zones, multinationals generally prefer single women. Pregnancy tests are routinely given to avoid maternity benefits. In the Philippines' Bataan Export Processing Zone, the Mattel toy company offered prizes to workers who underwent sterilisation. There have even been extreme cases documented where women were locked in for 23 hours out of 24 and given amphetamines to increase production.

Quite apart from the issue of workers' rights, the benefits of free trade zones to Third World countries are questionable. The companies operating there do not tend to use local materials or become part of the local economy. Governments receive very little in revenue. Intense competition to attract investment means that Third World countries are gaining less and less from it.

Bargaining
To decrease their vulnerability in the face of giant corporations, Third World countries need to increase their bargaining strength. The 1987 Bruntland Report on environment and development explains:

"Negotiations are often made one-sided by a developing

country's lack of information, technical unpreparedness, and political and institutional weakness.

"Strengthening the bargaining posture and response of Third World countries vis-à-vis transnationals is therefore critical. Where nations lack indigenous capacity to deal with large TNCs, regional and other international institutions should assist."

Common standards
Ideally, poor countries' bargaining positions could be strengthened if they worked together, not against each other. A set of common minimum standards, rather than the current 'beggar my neighbour' approach, would ensure higher returns. Third World trade blocs might help too. But the current economic difficulties of many countries which are in competition with each other for investment and markets means that co-ordination is likely to prove difficult.

Regulation
With fewer and bigger companies dominating the world market, they can, and often do, make more profit by informal co-ordination of their prices and products than

Christian Aid/David Hayes

Since women everywhere are paid less than men, they are the obvious choice for companies looking for cheap labour.

49

by open competition. In response, free trade requires periodic regulation in order to remain free. Monopoly laws in developed countries recognise this.

Yet there is no such regulation on an international scale, with nothing to stop monopolies building up or to deal with unfair practices (the GATT hardly recognises the existence of TNCs). As it is, if companies are threatened by regulation on the national level, they can pack up shop and move elsewhere.

A code of conduct for transnationals has been under discussion in the UN since 1974. This envisages rights and duties for both host countries and transnationals. But after years of negotiation and watering-down, any benefits are now doubtful.

Nor is the UN necessarily the right forum. TNCs are so central to the international economic system that regulation should also be at its centre. The most obvious organisation to undertake this would be the GATT or whatever organisation comes to replace it.

Consumer action

Major international companies are no more alike than the Third World countries they operate in. Some are much better in the way they treat these countries and their workers than others. One way to encourage them all to improve is for shoppers or shareholders to use their buying power to reward the good and punish the bad.

Consumer power can encourage companies to change their policies. This was shown in the boycott of Barclays Bank over its investment in South Africa. It is seen in the plethora of 'environmentally-friendly' products filling our supermarket shelves. Christian Aid has supported *The Global Consumer*, a book aimed at changing company practice through consumer pressure. The book provides detailed advice on how companies score on a range of issues. For example, we should buy from companies that have a policy of joint ventures with local firms and governments (which tends to mean greater technology transfer) rather than the exclusive use of subsidiary operations. Companies that adopt unified health and safety or pollution standards or central monitoring of wages should be preferred to those that adopt local standards and comply only with local laws.

Workers' action

Companies which have links stretching across the globe can effectively play one country's workers off against another's (American and Japanese car firms have done this between Britain and other European countries for example). It is important that workers develop their own parallel links.

An organisation which helps them to do this is TIE, the Transnational Information Exchange, which works to strengthen the contacts between workers at different points of the production chain.

Companies which have links stretching across the globe can effectively play one country's workers off against another's

---

Christian Aid funds the educational materials of the TIE cocoa programme, which, since 1986, has helped workers from all parts of the cocoa chain in all continents meet and learn about each other's lives and problems.

Workers at Cadbury's in Bournville have twinned with a Brazilian trade union branch. Dutch trade unionists are supporting the building up of trade union infrastructure in the Brazilian and Ghanaian cocoa regions.

These international networks allow for solidarity and more long-term strategies for workers. Dockers in Amsterdam felt dizzy and sick when unloading cocoa beans. Through international contacts they found the reason: highly toxic tablets were placed between the sacks to kill insects during transportation. After union protests, the use of these tablets has decreased.

If landowners or governments in cocoa-growing countries use violence or intimidation, European trade unionists will denounce this. When, in 1989, 925 trade union members were about to be sacked in the cocoa region of Bahia, Brazil, protest from European trade unions caused the company, worried about adverse publicity, to back down and re-instate the workers.

Spreading the gains from trade

TNCs, like everyone involved in trade, are in business to make a profit. They are not evil or immoral (although the pressure to make profits might force them to behave in that way) but nor are they in the business of helping anyone other than themselves. Only when the bargaining power of other sectors of society (such as workers or consumers) is increased are the benefits from trade likely

Spraying bananas with pesticides in the Philippines.

Christian Aid/Stuart Franklin

to spread.

Consider working conditions for example. Leonardo works on one of the large banana plantations in Mindanao in the Philippines, spraying bananas with insecticide. In order to refill the tank that he carries on his back, he scoops up the chemicals with his bare hands.

Leonardo and many of his friends have severe skin problems. Other workers, who handle more dangerous pesticides, have suffered more serious health damage, including sterility and blood poisoning.

Dangerous chemicals, many banned in Britain, are used at every stage of banana production. Early in the morning an aeroplane dusts, not only the crops, but the workers, their homes and local water supplies, with chemicals.

On pineapple, sugar, rubber and tobacco plantations all over Mindanao, there are similar cases. Most of these plantations are owned by large international companies which have been encouraged to make use of the cheap labour. For thousands of people there is no choice but to accept the low wages and dangerous working conditions on the plantations.

Christian Aid supports the National Federation of

Labour (NFL) which helps workers to improve their conditions. NFL have succeeded in obtaining minimum protective clothing for their members. Local union officials have helped workers set up health committees to learn about the dangers of the products they use and the necessary preventative measures. Clinics provide free emergency treatment.

Despite intense harassment, the Federation now represents nearly 40,000 workers in the Philippines. As Amado Magbanua, an NFL official put it, "We not only work for better wages and conditions, but for the benefit of the whole community."

A social clause

Trade unions, non-governmental organisations and human rights activists have repeatedly called for a charter of workers' rights to be built into trade agreements. This would protect against abuse and exploitation of workers by not allowing in goods that were produced under unacceptable working conditions.

A social clause would have several advantages. It would contribute to social and economic progress; it would also counteract unfair competition and keep social progress in step with economic development.

There is a danger, however, that it could be an excuse for protectionist measures by rich countries. In order to prevent it being used to keep out goods based on cheaper labour – which is the main advantage Third World countries have when it comes to trading – its criteria should be based on certain absolute standards rather than relative ones. These would include the right of association and the right to free collective bargaining.

The position of the poor can be improved by international action and regulation. There is a parallel here with 19th-century Britain. The response to the appalling conditions of factory workers was not to abolish factories. Instead it was, through the Factory Acts, to draw up a list of norms and regulations that all would follow. The same is true of trade. The answer is not to abolish it, but to draw up some minimum criteria. National standards are not enough; if production is international, regulation must be too.

CHAPTER FIVE

Building blocs

"When two elephants fight, it's always the grass that gets hurt."
African proverb

Every week the Geest company boat sails from the Caribbean Windward Island of Dominica to Britain, its refrigerated hold filled with boxes of unripe bananas which will eventually find their way to our shops and market stalls. Bananas – a pleasant fruit for us – are the main livelihood of Windward Islands' farmers.

The islands rely heavily on selling bananas to the UK for their export earnings (60 per cent in the case of Dominica). Geest is the only exporting company.

These bananas are usually grown on small plots of steep hill-side land, by poor farmers who receive a low, but fairly secure, price for their produce. Although no longer colonies of Europe, the people of these islands still depend for their livelihood on a continent 5,000 miles away.

The EC is the second largest banana importer in the world (after the US) and some of its members have special trading relationships with their ex-colonies through the Lomé Convention. Such preferences, as they are termed, have allowed the industry in the Windward Islands to survive, but have tended further to increase dependency.

As part of the new Single Market process, however, EC trade regulations will have to be harmonised, removing the special trading deals offered by individual countries. This threatens the Caribbean producers, because they cannot compete with the bananas grown on plantations in Central and South America.

The hilly terrain, small-scale production and labour rates make production costs about 30 per cent higher than for Latin American banana producers whose plantations are large, with flat land, good soil and a high degree of mechanisation. In addition, repressive conditions keep wages on the plantations very low. During pay negotiations in Colombia in 1987, over 200 people – mainly trade union leaders and plantation workers – were

Christian Aid/Philip Wolmuth

The people of Dominica in the Caribbean are dependent for their survival on exporting bananas to Europe.

55

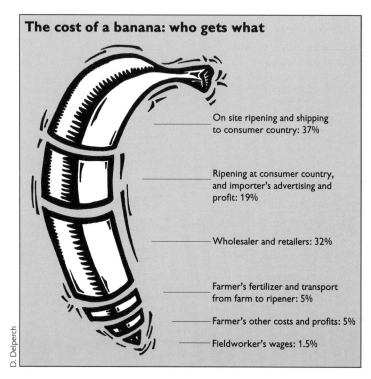

The cost of a banana: who gets what

On site ripening and shipping to consumer country: 37%

Ripening at consumer country, and importer's advertising and profit: 19%

Wholesaler and retailers: 32%

Farmer's fertilizer and transport from farm to ripener: 5%

Farmer's other costs and profits: 5%

Fieldworker's wages: 1.5%

D. Delperch

killed in the banana region of Urabá alone.

The four Windward Islands account for three out of every five bananas eaten in Britain and would face economic catastrophe were they to lose their market share.

It is not just the Caribbean that will be affected by changes in Europe. Just as the 'discovery' of the Americas had a dramatic impact and began a re-shaping of the world, in the 500th anniversary year changes are afoot that will also have profound consequences. The map of the world is again being re-drawn.

1992 and all that

Midnight on December 31, 1992 is the deadline for the completion of the Single Market in Europe.

The objective is a huge market without frontiers which will put Europe in a strong competitive position globally. It will have markets, multinational companies and a currency (the ECU) to rival those of the US and Japan. The physical, tax and technical barriers between the 12 member states will be removed.

The EC is already the largest trading bloc in the world,

with an internal market of 340 million people accounting for 37 per cent of world trade. It will increase in size still further as other countries join. Trade with Third World countries accounts for around one-third of European exports and imports.

The EC claim is that the 1992 process will be to everybody's benefit. Growth in Europe will increase demand for raw materials and other imports from Third World countries. There will be no 'Fortress Europe', closed to the outside world. Instead, it is argued, the Single Market will mean more simple and streamlined import procedures, which should benefit poor countries.

The balance sheet
The precise nature of the impact of Europe 1992 on the Third World has yet to be seen. But some broad brush-strokes can be painted. In the short term, the host of new standards, rules and regulations which are to be introduced will mean that without help and information, poor countries will find it even harder to get into Europe.

Most of the economic forecasting sees the costs and benefits to poor countries balancing out overall, but this ignores the differing impacts on certain countries and products. The EC Director for Development admits: "Japan will be better able to seize these opportunities than Senegal and, among the developing countries, South Korea will be better placed than Burkina Faso."

Producers with special deals will also be hard hit and African countries in particular stand to be further marginalised. The lack of care or consultation on the impact of the Single Market does not augur well (the Single European Act did not mention Third World countries). This situation is compounded by changes in eastern Europe. Because of geographical proximity, cultural similarities and political ideals, Europe is likely to concentrate aid and attention there at the Third World's expense.

This was evident in 1991 when EC Ministers gave political priority to food aid for the former Soviet Union and had to be persuaded (by Christian Aid and others) that the needs of millions facing starvation in Africa were greater.

The EC will have even greater power too to use its immense size to make demands on Third World countries, as it has done recently on the newly independent country of Namibia.

Namibia's valuable mineral and marine resources were

heavily over-exploited under South African rule. Between 1976 and 1980, hake quantities were reduced by more than half, while the pilchard stock fell to just two per cent of its previous level.

After independence in 1990, the new government took steps to protect its shores by setting up a 200 mile Economic Exclusion Zone. However this was repeatedly ignored, largely by Spanish vessels. When the Namibian government seized some boats and arrested their crews, the EC Fisheries Commissioner Manuel Marin, himself a Spaniard, broke off negotiations between Namibia and the EC on a future fisheries agreement.

Processes paralleling Europe 1992 are taking place in other parts of the world. Three great trading blocs are growing up

---

The EC is in a strong position, offering Third World countries badly-needed foreign exchange in return for access to their waters. But for the latter, there are other priorities, such as conservation and the development of indigenous fishing fleets and processing industries. These require more equitable agreements based on co-operation and assistance, moving the emphasis away from the short-term profits of EC member states to the longer term social and economic development of countries like Namibia.

Other blocs

Processes paralleling Europe 1992 are taking place in other parts of the world. Three great trading blocs are growing up: in Europe (the EC with other countries trying to join), the US, Canada and Mexico bloc, and possibly Japan, Australasia and the western Pacific.

The US already has a free trade agreement with Canada and is at present negotiating with Mexico. In the longer term this bloc might include the countries of Central and South America. President Bush advocates a free trade zone stretching from Alaska to Tierra del Fuego.

Competition between these blocs and a retreat into bilateralism and 'tit for tat' protectionism would have severe consequences for the Third World. Agricultural wars between the US and the EC during the 1980s are evidence of the damage that can be done.

Argentina has been buffeted by rich countries'

agricultural policies. As a beef exporter it lost an important export market when Britain joined the EC in the 1970s. It was then out-priced in markets outside Europe as a result of the dumping of heavily subsidised European beef. At the end of the 1980s it had to stop exports of sugar – although it had been one of the ten largest sugar exporters in the world – because of rock-bottom world prices caused by over-production in the EC and import restrictions in the US.

Argentina's exports of wheat and maize, which formed half of the country's export earnings, have suffered heavily from the subsidy war between the US and EC. The resulting drop in earnings from export taxes has caused government revenue to fall by 70 per cent.

These emerging blocs are part of the changing pattern of trade which is likely to have negative implications for Third World countries. A two tier system is developing in the world. There are the more advanced countries (a handful of which, such as Mexico, are in the Third World), many of which are becoming involved in regional trading blocs. A number of other countries which are nearby or have strong historical ties may derive some benefit from the formation of these blocs. Others will not fit in anywhere. There is a danger that the weakest countries (particularly those of sub-Saharan Africa) will become completely marginalised.

A two tier system is developing in the world... There is a danger that the weakest countries will become completely marginalised

The costs of entering more sophisticated markets, where power, size and global marketing networks are more important sources of comparative advantage, are continually rising. As certain countries get left behind it will become harder and harder for them to break through.

Trade between poor countries

How should poor countries respond to these developments? Firstly they should argue, with our support, for continued and improved access to rich countries' markets. They also need information, support and compensation for problems caused by the formation of these trading blocs. At the same time they might develop their own trading blocs. It is dangerous to rely too much on the goodwill of rich countries.

This would be a logical response to the trends outlined above. It would reduce dependency on rich countries and encourage development strategies that are more equitable and more suited to local conditions.

Only four per cent of Africa's trade is carried out within the continent

Third World blocs would also act as a counterbalance to the political and economic weight of the groupings of rich countries, provide a measure of self sufficiency and spread risks.

But trade between poor countries has been declining. Only four per cent of Africa's trade is carried out within the continent.

According to Hans Singer of the Institute of Development Studies: "It is an anomaly that the 75 per cent of the world's population who live in Third World countries should only do some seven per cent of their world trade with each other whereas the 12 per cent of the world's population living in the Western industrialised countries should do over 79 per cent with each other. There is no economic rhyme or reason for this...the reasons are political, financial and institutional."

Despite the failure of Third World blocs in the past, they have been given a renewed impetus by the changing pattern of global trade, and a number of initiatives are emerging. These are not without problems for some of the people in them, particularly in view of a lack of the type of regional compensation funds which exist in the EC. In the long run, however, if the right emphases emerge within the blocs, they should result in more strength for the peoples of the Third World.

The Association of South East Asian Nations has announced the setting up of a free trade area with the explicit aim of countering the emerging powerful trading blocs of Europe and North America. This area would create a market of more than 320 million consumers. In South America, Brazil, Argentina, Paraguay and Uruguay are joining together in their own trading bloc called 'Mercosur'.

For the poorer countries it is much more difficult to form such groupings. Lack of adequate communications and transport systems are a major problem; most of these were designed to transport products to rich countries, not as a basis for regional trade.

Many countries have very similar export structures, making it hard for them to work together, and lack internal markets. Political conflicts are a further stumbling block, particularly when one country in the region is economically very dominant.

These problems are particularly acute for sub-Saharan Africa, although there may be new hope for the countries of southern Africa working with a post-apartheid South Africa along the lines pioneered by the Southern African Development Co-ordination Conference (SADCC).

Given the great disparities in economic development and living standards in the region, a co-ordination of efforts could promote a more balanced development than a focus on growth alone, which would probably increase inequalities.

Europe has helped to create dependency and should now support diversification and regional common markets. This would not only include funding institutions at sub-regional, regional and inter-regional levels, but also providing the credit and finance to allow developing countries to trade among themselves.

Just as Christian Aid sees it as vital to strengthen the poor at a local, community level, so increasing the bargaining power of poor countries on the world scale will be equally important in ensuring a better return from trade.

CHAPTER SIX

Christian ethics and trade

"Despite all the advance of the 20th century, more than one billion people, a fifth of the world's population, live on less than one dollar a day; a standard of living that Western Europe and the US attained 200 years ago."

The World Bank World Development Report, 1991

The unfolding story of trade reveals how the international economic system, sometimes by accident, sometimes by design, contributes to global poverty and inequality. How should Christians respond to this?

When they are faced with economic and political issues of this kind there are broadly two temptations Christians should resist. The first is to back away from them, retreat into the private sphere and see the moral aspects of Christianity as essentially personal, concentrating on the relationship between the individual and God in the hope that enough godly individuals will change the world for good.

Such a retreat is understandable in many ways. The issues are complex. The gap between them and religious faith seems hard to bridge. Many of the people involved, whether poor people in the Third World or the policy makers on the international scene, are far away. But if we set out to love our neighbours and act in ways that will generally serve their interests and not just ours, then we cannot ignore the systems which so radically affect their lives for good or ill.

The second temptation is to apply moral or religious insights over-directly to economic and political issues, to 'read off' from Christian scripture and tradition precepts for the contemporary world, forgetting that there are many other considerations to be taken into account.

How then should our religious faith and moral values on the one hand engage with the political and economic issues involved in international trade on the other? For Christians it will mean first of all being clear about the moral values they wish to uphold, drawing on the Bible, Christian faith and the insights gained over centuries of practical Christian experience and moral argument. They will also have to seek wider moral agreement because no international order can operate as if only Christians are involved.

When it comes to trade, four obvious examples of moral values (and the list is by no means complete) would be that everyone: should have a reasonable standard of living with access to what they need; should receive a reasonable return for their work without exploiting others; should live in structures of family, economic and political life which foster a communal sense of mutual responsibility; and should have a measure of freedom and opportunity to control their own lives and decide and pursue what they regard as good for them.

Of course these basic examples beg as many questions as they raise. What, for example, is a reasonable standard of living? What is exploitation? How do we reconcile our individual freedom with the responsibilities of living together in a community?

Nevertheless, we can uphold these and other values in the sense that whatever we do should at least have a bias in their favour. It should promote them and not frustrate or deny them.

For Christians it will mean first of all being clear about the moral values they wish to uphold, drawing on the Bible, Christian faith and the insights gained over centuries of practical Christian experience and moral argument

---

Once these moral values have been clarified they cannot be upheld without coming to terms with reality, otherwise we shall not 'love' our neighbours in any meaningful sense. Instead we shall only sentimentally wish the best for them without effectively achieving it.

It is important to be realistic about human nature. Although human beings are capable of being generous towards each other and disregarding themselves, more often than not they behave in highly selfish (if often

Chris Steele-Perkins/Christian Aid

Streamlining to maximise market potential can have immense social costs. The unemployed in Chile still have to scrape a living.

short-sighted) ways. They tend to love themselves and not their neighbours, and even more so when they get together in organised groups and nations.

We should, therefore, not expect them to respond to moral appeals to ensure that their neighbours have a decent standard of living and a fair wage. We have to regulate and legislate for the likelihood that they will not.

Power and poverty

At this point issues of power become extremely important: especially economic and political power. This is another area from which Christians too often stand aloof, perhaps because of the ambiguities of power or because its exercise does not seem easy to reconcile with devotion to a 'powerless' Jesus. But if we are serious about a fair deal for the poor, then we have to pay attention to their power and to our own. We have to increase their ability to stand up to those with power, wealth and influence who, left to themselves, will usually do them down. They may be the socially or economically powerful within their own communities and countries, or their own or foreign governments, or international trading corporations or financial institutions. Such a strategy to match power more equally with power and so avoid the worst of injustice, lies behind Christian Aid's fundamental commitment 'to strengthen the poor'.

We cannot expect our governments and business institutions to respond to the needs of the poor out of the kindness of their hearts. We have to use our own power as consumers and citizens in a democracy to persuade them to change inadequate policies.

If we are serious about a fair deal for the poor, then we have to pay attention to their power and to our own

---

Another aspect of coming to terms with the real world and another reason why we cannot simply read-off political or economic policies from our Christian convictions, it is that our loving actions need to be effective rather than merely sentimental. We shall want to argue for policies which actually work, and this is where the economists, for example, will have an indispensable role to play.

The role of experts

If politics is chiefly to do with establishing and pursuing the policies which shape the sort of society we want – in this case, one in which the opportunity to earn and enjoy a decent standard of living is open to us all – then economics is one of the disciplines which attempts to make those policies work.

Economics is about using available resources as efficiently as possible to provide people with what they need and want. Achieving this, or rather creating the economic systems such as industries and markets that will deliver it, is not only difficult but highly technical. Some things will work and others will not. Different values such as freedom and justice may be difficult to hold together in one system. There will be trade-offs. The competition required by efficiency in an economic sense may be hard to reconcile with the moralist's demand for justice. Christians must learn from economics, respect the difficulties and technicalities and accept that we cannot do what cannot be done.

Having brought their values to the economic experts and respecting what is sometimes called the 'autonomy' of the economist's discipline – its ability to say things on its own account – Christians will not however fulfil their moral obligations simply by accepting what the experts say, even though they will take what they say very seriously indeed.

They will continue to press their case for a number of reasons. One is because experts, not least economists, disagree with one another. We should not accept too easily that something cannot be done or that it can only be done in one way. Second, we should be watchful about the way in which it is proposed to do it, since the end does not always justify the means; thirdly, since economists are human like the rest of us, what they suggest and settle for can never be perfect and can always be improved; and finally, it is important to remember also that economic judgements are not usually 'value free'. Consciously or unconsciously they may represent certain vested interests. Expert advisers are not necessarily more independent than anyone else.

The market

Some of these points can be illustrated by looking at the market. With the collapse of the Soviet system, market-based economics are seen by many as the only model on offer. Disputes now centre on the market, what it can and cannot achieve, how much or little regulation it requires, and around the ideology that accompanies it; but less on the market itself.

The market has obvious benefits. It is a highly efficient way of maximising the productivity of relatively scarce resources and of getting economic decisions made while leaving the consumer with freedom of choice. In our increasingly complex societies it allows a great deal of flexibility. It matches supply and demand. To this extent it 'works'.

We cannot do without markets, but nor can we do with them alone. On their own they tend to reproduce cumulative inequalities of income and power. We have seen how difficult it is for new industries in the Third World to break into them. Here there is genuine disagreement among 'experts' as to whether a lowering of tariffs and trade barriers will on balance stimulate and so benefit Third World producers or do them down.

Markets are not good at providing public services or universal access to them. If they are sensitive to demand, they are insensitive to social costs. The imposition of neo-liberal, market-based systems in Third World countries during the 1980s has led to increases in hunger, unemployment and illiteracy. Nor are markets able to deal with environmental costs. These fall outside traditional accounting systems. Once taken into account they can undermine a firm's competitive position. Again markets are not good at long-term planning.

Paradoxically then, in order to function successfully, the 'free' market needs strong and continual regulation. If it is to uphold some of our moral values it cannot be left to itself. It must do its work within a social and political order and that order, given the global nature of present trading systems, has to be of international dimensions.

If in our view the present trading system contributes to keeping a large part of the world's people in poverty, then Christian love requires that it be changed. And it can be changed; but to do so we need to be clear about the moral values we wish to uphold; what will work for the good of poor people, enabling them to earn a living, and what will not; and how we and they can gain and exercise power to achieve a more just system of trade.

CHAPTER SEVEN

A new deal

"The international trading system was devised by the rich to suit their needs; it ignores those of the poor."
Pope Paul VI

How can the world trading system be changed from one which pushes the poor to the sidelines to one which strengthens their ability to develop?

Christian Aid cannot offer blanket prescriptions, nor a blueprint for economic success in every Third World country. It can, however, outline the sorts of changes that would make the trading system fairer. It is under no illusion that these changes are enough to eradicate poverty, but they will begin the important process of making the way we trade of benefit to all.

Successful trading depends on the interaction between a country's own economic strategy and the world economy – every case is different. The Third World ranges from desperately poor countries such as Burkina Faso and Niger to relatively developed ones such as Hong Kong and South Korea. Some countries, like these so-called 'Asian Tigers', have scored remarkable successes in world trade. Others, especially those in sub-Saharan Africa, are becoming more and more marginalised. It is clear that a trade policy based more on concepts of justice and need would have to take account of these differences.

Some of the more developed Third World countries, such as Mexico or Brazil, are in a position to fend for themselves and compete successfully if abuses are prevented and the strong trading nations are stopped from exploiting the weak. Others require special treatment to compensate for marginalisation from the system and to help them overcome structural barriers to development such as commodity dependence.

A fairer deal

We have seen how rich countries are far more protectionist in their dealings with poor countries than they are with each other. This is particularly acute in those areas where the Third World might realistically break into a more modern and dynamic role – such as processed agricultural products (instant coffee, orange juice), shoes and textiles. The economic costs of this protectionism exceed the aid given by rich countries.

Some of the more developed Third World countries are in a position to fend for themselves and compete successfully if abuses are prevented and the strong trading nations are stopped from exploiting the weak

---

We have also seen how poor countries are opening up their markets to foreign imports while at the same time rich countries are becoming increasingly protectionist. The extent to which the new trading blocs, such as the European Single Market, will increase this trend, remains to be seen.

Poor countries cannot be expected to open up their markets any further for the time being until they have been given concessions for the measures they have taken during the 1980s. Strategic barriers such as tariffs should remain in place in order to protect food security and fledgling industries. The removal of barriers should be based on clear benefits: whether through a process of bargaining for parallel agreements in other countries or because production can cope with, and benefit from, the stimulus of international competition.

While rich countries are preaching free trade they cling to agricultural subsidies which cost billions of pounds – a cost born by us as tax-payers and consumers as well as by the Third World. Mazide Ndiaye, Director of RADI, an organisation supported by Christian Aid in Senegal, describes how: "At this moment the market is flooded by potatoes, onions and the like from abroad, mainly France and the Netherlands, which are cheaper than Senegalese. I am not against liberalisation, but a young economy has a right to be protected. You subsidise your farmers in Europe, whereas we are not allowed to subsidise under our structural adjustment programme."

All too often there is one rule for the weak and another for the strong.

The trading system needs rules by which everyone, including the strong, will abide, and a body to enforce them. The GATT is likely to be strengthened or replaced after the current round of negotiations. The best option would be to replace it with a new ITO. If the more modest European proposal for a Multilateral Trade Organisation goes ahead, this should also be democratic and accountable and have the power to bring the US, EC and Japan (and their major international companies) to account.

It might be argued that such a 'levelling of the playing field' is unfair to the rich countries because wages, conditions and standards of living are so low in poor ones; allowing open competition would drive down standards in rich countries as well.

One obvious way around this dilemma is the idea of a social clause in trading agreements to ensure better wages and working conditions. This makes sense from an ethical point of view (it would help to spread the gains from trade). It would also go some way to reassuring workers in the rich, industrialised countries. If the cheapness of goods from the Third World is based on gross exploitation of labour, this discriminates against socially progressive regimes elsewhere.

But the answer is not to keep such goods out – that would only make conditions even worse. It is to use trade policy to encourage better working conditions.

Equal treatment today does not compensate for unequal treatment in the past. Indeed, it is likely to intensify inequalities

---

A special deal

Even in a system based more squarely on rules, some countries will still need special help to overcome structural problems or historical weaknesses which are partly the fault of rich countries. Equal treatment today does not compensate for unequal treatment in the past. Indeed, it is likely to intensify inequalities.

Some countries already receive special treatment – prominent is the EC's Lomé agreement for African, Caribbean and Pacific (ACP) countries. Valuable as they are, many of these special deals are hedged with difficulties, and some are under threat from the latest round of GATT talks and the Single Market in Europe. It is vital that they are not removed without other provisions being made. Third World countries which have become reliant on them need help in transition, including special packages of assistance, aid and debt relief.

Recognising that the poorest countries need special help does not mean that they should shy away entirely from the world market – that would prove very damaging in the long run. But nor should they be thrown to the wolves.

Differential treatment is especially vital in agriculture, since food security and a flourishing and widespread agricultural base provide such an important platform for development.

Rich countries have only belatedly begun to address the debt crisis. They must turn their attention also to the commodity crisis, which has been of equal severity

---

The very poorest countries which depend for most of their export earnings on raw materials need realistic prices which at least cover production costs. Rich countries have only belatedly begun to address the debt crisis. They must turn their attention also to the commodity crisis, which has been of equal severity.

Stabilisation of prices on a year to year basis would help poor countries and producers deal with wild fluctuations. The general aim would be to provide a measure of stability rather than maintain prices at an artificially high level. But some prices do need to be higher in order to reflect the full social and environmental costs of production.

Production agreements among producers would be a good start. The World Bank should not weaken this co-ordination (as it did with palm oil), but should encourage it. The International Coffee Agreement, which used to regulate production and quality, is due for renegotiation in 1993. It is to be hoped that this will pave the way for a new era of co-operation on commodities.

The poorest countries need help to move away from commodity dependence. Lower tariffs on processed goods would allow countries to do more of their own processing. They would also benefit from support for diversifying their exports backed up by credit and investment. Aid for specific products and specific regions is the answer – especially for sub-Saharan Africa. The EC should support the African countries' recent proposal of a diversification fund for their continent outlined in the UN Programme of Action for African Economic Recovery and Development.

Financing fairer trade

Trade and production need money invested in them. Countries and communities in the Third World are desperately short of this, and the debt crisis has sucked them even drier. Policies to increase investment which benefit the poor are vital, both at the local and international level.

Christian Aid supports such work at the local level, providing finance and supporting small-scale credit for example. Unfortunately, aid is not always as effective at government to government level.

Aid from European countries is inadequate and often inappropriate. Much of it, for example, is tied to the purchase of goods and services from the countries giving it. These tend to be from declining industries or those of strategic interest to rich countries, rather than goods that will help the development process.

Aid should support development by encouraging trade between communities and countries in the Third World. If the World Bank was to fund Export Credit Guarantee Institutions, these could provide the finance for trade between Third World countries.

European countries could help still further by increasing aid and untying it from the condition to buy their goods. They could build on the moves to cancel Third World debt, such as John Major's 'Trinidad Terms' which write-off two-thirds of the debt owed by the poorest countries. For this is the paradox: without investment the poor cannot trade and without successful trade there is likely to be another debt crisis.

Changes in the Third World

But it would be foolish for the Third World to rely entirely on rich countries' good will. Such countries have not hesitated to manipulate the system to their own advantage. The Third World needs to take its own steps to balance the power of rich nations.

Where commodities are concerned, this means working together, not against each other, if the many producers are to have any impact on the few major international companies there are in this area. Third World countries will also have to work to balance the power of these companies more generally, developing bargaining power and setting agreed standards and positions where possible.

They need to move away from heavy dependence on exports of single commodities to rich countries and into regional trade.

In the Caribbean, the future of banana growers in the Windward Islands is under threat from the Single European Market. Although the farmers need to start moving into other crops, they are understandably wary about abandoning banana cultivation, which has guaranteed them a living.

Nor are the governments of the Windward Islands eager to act, fearing that any shift will make them deeply unpopular. So there is a tendency to carry on with their heads in the sand.

One group that is taking action is the Small Projects Assistance Team (SPAT), a group supported by Christian Aid, which is helping small farmers move away from banana dependence. It provides technology and training, and researches marketing opportunities for other products.

Instead of exporting bananas to earn money to import food, farmers can grow local staple foods themselves

Developing a secure food supply is an important part of this work. Instead of exporting bananas to earn money to import food, farmers can grow local staple foods themselves. Ninety nine per cent of the chicken eaten on Dominica is imported, so there is plenty of room for domestic production. SPAT has also identified a great potential for agricultural exports to other Caribbean countries, because many of them concentrate on tourism. Spices are grown too for the US market.

SPAT hopes that by demonstrating that there are viable alternatives to bananas they will get other farmers to follow suit, and will influence government policy as well. This will take time, so Christian Aid is lobbying for EC banana preferences to be maintained during a transitional period of 15 years.

Elites who reap the greatest benefits from trade, exploitative companies and corrupt bureaucracies contribute a major barrier to fairer trade

---

As Third World communities and countries share information and work together, they can develop home and regional markets. They could also help each other to gain a better price on imports, instead of ending up with expensive and inappropriate goods because of lack of information and bargaining power, which often happens at the moment. A recent World Bank and IMF report showed that the African countries had paid large premiums for imports from their former colonisers. Former French colonies, for instance, had paid an average premium of 24 per cent between 1962 and 1987 for iron and steel imports. The cost to the countries were in some cases equivalent to their foreign debts.

Trade for the poor
Vested interests must be tackled in poor countries as well as rich ones. Elites who reap the greatest benefits from trade, exploitative companies and corrupt bureaucracies contribute a major barrier to fairer trade.

Non-governmental organisations and trade unions in the Third World have a vital role to play here. Christian Aid supports such work all over the world.

Since the Israeli occupation of the West Bank and Gaza began, the practice of drawing the territories into an extended Israeli economy has created severe disruption to traditional agriculture and land use. Cheap Israeli produce dumped on the Palestinian market has undermined producers and the Israeli government has made independent exports by Palestinians extremely difficult.

Christian Aid is supporting the Palestinian Agricultural Relief Committee (PARC) to help small farmers export agricultural produce from the West Bank. Most of the profit for almonds, for example, a traditional crop, is made by commission agents. PARC will give local farmers a better deal by finding direct export markets for them. Almonds and nut butter will soon be on sale in the UK through the alternative trade organisations Equal Exchange and Traidcraft.

In the Philippines, the price of rice is largely controlled

Christian Aid is helping Palestinian farmers in the West Bank to export their traditional products.

by a cartel of merchants which pays farmers low prices and charges consumers more.

But the cartel is being challenged by Grassroots, an alternative trading organisation supported by Christian Aid, which offers peasants a better price for their crop and sells to slum-dwellers at below the usual rate. It can afford to do this because it refuses to make the kind of profits enjoyed by the cartel. Rice is collected and milled by Grassroots, then distributed to community organisations for selling.

In partnership with organisations like Grassroots, Christian Aid is helping the poor to work together to win a better deal – as both producers and consumers. This vision of trade is giving a fair return for labour, fulfilling basic needs, and strengthening the poor.

The same principles need to be applied at the international level. Christian Aid supports initiatives to give a fairer deal from trade, and you can be part of this too.

Alternative trade

The idea of fair trade is not just a pipe dream. A growing number of fair trade groups are demonstrating how day-to-day shopping decisions can make a difference.

Organisations like Traidcraft, Equal Exchange, Oxfam Trading, and TWIN Trading can change the lives of both producers and consumers. The former get a better deal for their labour and the latter come to realise that there is a human story behind every product they buy.

Just south of Calcutta, in an area where 70 per cent of the people are below the poverty line and 60 per cent are without land, Christian Aid works with the Sundarban Khadi and Village Industrial Society (SKVIS), a sewing and tailoring co-operative.

Without any help or advice from outside agencies, a group of women from poorly-educated and low-caste families started to sew for the local market. This meant doing jobs that were the traditional preserve of men, so they struggled to succeed at first. But, through the skilful development of both domestic and export markets, the society quickly grew to cover 20 villages and now has about 300 members.

The beautiful handmade fabrics the women produce are on sale in Europe and the USA, and can be bought through Traidcraft and Traidéireann (Ireland).

Traidcraft buys from over 200 such groups in more than 30 Third World countries. Its policy is to buy from sources which give workers a better deal and pursue responsible social policies. It pays a fair price and where appropriate, gives help with the design and marketing of new products.

Nonetheless, however valuable, such alternative trade is always likely to be the tip of an iceberg, a niche market. One of the problems is that far fewer people buy fair trade products than would actually like to, because it is too difficult to get hold of them. Only as consumer demand increases, as it has for 'green' products which are now readily available, will fair trade be brought out of the catalogues and side streets and into the supermarkets.

In Holland, the Max Havelaar seal of approval has shown this can be done. This is given to commercial coffee brands which meet ethical criteria based on fair trading, and today these are available in 90 per cent of the supermarkets in the country.

Christian Aid/Achinto Bhadra

The women of the Sundarban Khadi Village Industrial Society in India earn money and improve their status by producing fabrics for domestic and export markets.

Max Havelaar coffee takes around three per cent of the Dutch market – a small but significant share, given how much is spent on advertising coffee.

One reason is that it tastes good too. Taste tests have

regularly rated it higher than established brands. The idea is spreading to Belgium and France and a similar cocoa and chocolate initiative will be launched in Holland in 1992.

This success has encouraged the launch of the UK's first Fair Trade Mark later this year. A fair trade seal will be given to goods such as tea, coffee or honey which meet certain standards. These will be available in ordinary shops and supermarkets, making it easier to support fair trade.

The Fair Trade Mark should help to persuade commercial companies that it can make commercial sense to consider people as well as profits.

Traidcraft has recently been alerting consumers to the appalling conditions under which many of the clothes on sale in this country are produced, asking them, for example, if they would buy garments made by a woman locked in a Bangladeshi factory 23 hours a day. It has also been calling on the main clothes retailers here to adopt a code of practice to ensure the clothes they supply measure up as far as working conditions are concerned. Littlewoods stores have now gone public with such a code for its product buyers.

Companies which act in this way deserve our support. As well as the money we give to charity (one per cent of our incomes on average), we need to start using the economic power we can wield with the other 99 per cent.

The average child leaving school this year in the UK will spend around a million pounds during his or her lifetime. Since about 100 companies dominate the market for the top 20 consumer products from the Third World, it should be possible to change policies in the interests of both producers and consumers.

As Anwar Fazal of the International Organisation of Consumer Unions in Malaysia says: "The act of buying is a vote for an economic and social system, for a particular way of producing goods. We cannot ignore the conditions under which products are made – the environmental impact and working conditions. We are linked to them and we have a responsibility for them." In other words, as well as being part of the problem we can be part of the solution.

The way forward

The 1980s were a 'lost decade' for most Third World countries. Millions of people saw their living standards fall. By 1995 more than 400 million Africans, 55 per cent of the population, will be living below the poverty line. In Latin America 25 per cent of the population is unable to feed itself adequately and that number is rapidly increasing. In India 40 per cent of people in towns and 51 per cent in rural areas go hungry. Every year, more than 14 million children under the age of five continue to die because of poverty. For too many people things are getting worse, not better.

The trading system played a major part in this: commodity prices plummeted; subsidised and protected agriculture in rich countries pushed down world prices; these countries also increased protectionism generally; and the poor in the Third World bore the brunt of programmes which encouraged them to open up their markets.

Action is needed to prevent the situation getting worse for so many communities in the Third World. If it is to improve, it will require an even greater effort.

Christian Aid believes in long-term development which will allow the poor to stand on their own feet. Aid alone is not enough. Trade policies must also be changed.

1992 heralded important dates – the deadline for the completion of the Single Market in Europe and the anniversary that marked five centuries since Columbus landed in the Caribbean. This spurred the process of colonisation and exploitation which underlies many of today's problems. The coincidence of these two dates could mark a new beginning for the new Europe and its trading partners around the world.

Recommendations

Christian Aid recommends that the UK and Irish governments and the EC press for the following changes:

Protectionism

● The reduction of EC tariffs on Third World goods and the removal of tariffs that rise according to the level of processing.

● The unconditional phasing out of the Multi Fibre Arrangement, with support for those countries and communities which will experience difficulties in transition.

● The removal of export subsidies on agriculture by rich countries. Agricultural products should not be sold on the world market at below their production price.

Compensation

● More EC help for African, Caribbean and Pacific countries to diversify away from commodity dependence. This would be a necessary parallel to any reduction in trading preferences as a result of Europe 1992 and should include provision of information.

● World Bank funding for institutions to finance trade between Third World countries.

Regulation

● The setting up of a new regulatory body for trade, based on one member one vote, transparent decision-making procedures and the power to bring the US, EC and Japan to account.

● Stopping multilateral agencies like the World Bank from encouraging commodity exports; this increases global gluts and pushes down prices.

● The regulation of major international corporations by the GATT or the new regulatory body that replaces it. This should include rules on technology transfer.

● Social clauses for minimum working conditions based on the right of association and to free collective bargaining. This should be applied to all countries.

What you can do

● Find out more about world trade. Learn about where the products we use come from and how they are produced.

● Use your choices as a consumer, investor or citizen to support fairer trade. Buy fairly traded goods from groups such as Traidcraft.

● Help Christian Aid to strengthen the work of poor communities. Your money is needed, and so is your voice.

● Write to Christian Aid for a free copy of the Trade Pack and a list of resources on trade.

Glossary of trade terms

ACP
The 69 African, Caribbean and Pacific countries which, as former colonies of European nations, have a special trade relationship with the **EC** through the **Lomé Convention**.

Cartel
An organisation of producers controlling and co-ordinating their output in order to raise prices and profits.

Commodities
In this book, the raw materials or unprocessed products such as coffee, copper, cocoa or rubber supplied by the Third World. Commodity dependence describes over-reliance on these raw materials because of lack of alternatives to export.

Comparative advantage
The idea that countries should specialise in the products they can produce most cheaply and then trade with others for the things they need.

Diversification
Moving away from reliance on a limited number of raw materials to producing new products and thus spreading risks and increasing returns.

EC
The European Community, established under the Treaty of Rome in 1958, aims to reduce internal barriers to trade and thus increase prosperity. It currently has 12 members with at least another half a dozen countries eager to join.

Free trade zones
Also known as export processing zones, are areas set up in the Third World to encourage **TNCs** to settle and produce for export. They usually have tax breaks, subsidies and no trade union agreements.

GATT
The General Agreement on Tariffs and Trade, set up in 1947 to reduce tariffs and other barriers to free trade. More than 100 nations are now signatories.

GDP
Gross Domestic Product – the value of all the goods and services produced in a country in a year.

GNP
Gross National Product – **GDP** plus income from investments abroad and minus income taken out by foreign investors.

ICA
International Commodity Agreements, designed to stabilise commodity prices or raise prices, through production quotas and price support.

IMF
The International Monetary Fund, set up in 1944 in order to regulate the world's monetary system and make sure that big imbalances do not occur.

ITO
An International Trading Organisation. This was suggested after World War Two as one of three international organisations, the other two were the **World Bank** and **IMF**.

LDC
One of 43 United Nations-defined Least Developed Countries which have very low incomes and levels of industrialisation.

Lomé Convention
Originally signed in 1975 and renewed approximately every five years, regulates the trade access to the **EC** of 69 **ACP** countries, mostly former colonies.

MFA
The Multi Fibre Arrangement, established in 1974 to protect rich countries from Third World competition in textiles by limiting imports. It restricts textile imports from developing countries, but not from industrialised ones.

MFN
Most Favoured Nation. Each member of **GATT** must treat all other members as well as it treats its most favoured trading partner.

Neo-liberalism
An economic (and hence political) philosophy espoused by Thatcher and Reagan and now being implemented in many Third World countries. It is characterised by a faith in markets, distrust of economic intervention by the state, privatisation, deregulation and the opening of markets.

NICs
Newly industrialised countries such as South Korea or Singapore.

NTBs
Non-Tariff Barriers, a variety of indirect restrictions on imports, such as quotas, **VERs** and anti-dumping measures.

OECD
The Organisation for Economic Co-operation and Development, made up of the 20 major industrialised Western nations.

Protectionism
The restriction of imports through, eg **tariffs** in order to protect domestic industries.

Single European Market
The removal of trading, physical and tax barriers between the members of the **EC** which is supposed to happen by the end of 1992.

Structural Adjustment Programmes
SAPs are a package of economic reform measures that Third World countries are forced to undertake by the **IMF**. A typical package would include increasing exports, cutting government expenditure, devaluing the currency and abolishing import and price controls.

Substitution
The replacement of a commodity by another commodity or synthetic substitute, eg plastic for copper pipes, nutrasweet for sugar.

Tariff
A fixed percentage tax (eg 30 per cent) on the value of an imported good levied at the point of entry into the importing country.

Tariff escalation
The more processed the product, the higher the tariff. When imported into the **EC**, fresh pineapples attract a duty of nine per cent, canned pineapples 32 per cent and pineapple juice 42 per cent.

Terms of trade
The ratio of a country's average export price to its average import price. A country's terms of trade worsen when this ratio decreases, ie when import prices rise at a faster rate than export prices.

TNC
Transnational corporations – large companies which operate in more than one country.

UNCTAD
The United Nations Conference on Trade and Development, a body of the UN established in 1962, whose main objective is to promote international trade and commerce with a principal focus on the problems of developing nations.

Uruguay Round
The current round of **GATT** negotiations, begun in 1986.

VER
Voluntary Export Restraint. Voluntary in the Mafia sense, the **EC** uses threats of other measures to force countries to restrict exports.

World Bank
Set up in 1944, one of its main objectives is to promote Third World development by providing funds and technical assistance.

Further reading

The Trade Trap: Poverty and the Global Commodity Markets
Belinda Coote, Oxfam, 1992.

The South on the World Market
Jan Kluglist et al, HIVOS, NCOS, NIO and NOVIB, 1991.
Available from:
Novib, Amaliastraat 7, 2514 JC The Hague, Netherlands.

Poverty and the Planet
Ben Jackson, Penguin 1990.

EC Trade Policy and the Third World: an Irish Perspective
Alan Matthews, Trocaire/Gill and MacMillan, 1991.

Hungry Farmers
Clive Robinson, Christian Aid, 1989.

The Global Consumer
Phil Wells and Mandy Jetter, Victor Gollancz, 1991.

Fair trade organisations

Equal Exchange
29 Nicholson Street, Edinburgh EH8 9BX
Specialises in foods from the Third World.

Ethical Consumer
100 Gretney Walk
Manchester, M15 5ND
Publishes a bi-monthly magazine on ethical shopping.

The Fair Trade Foundation
c/o **New Consumer**
Runs the Fair Trade Mark scheme.

The Irish Fair Trade Network
c/o **Christian Aid**
Christ Church, Rathgar Road, Dublin 6
Co-ordinates practical and educational work on fair trade.

New Consumer
52 Elswick Road, Newcastle upon Tyne NE4 6JH
Publishes books and a quarterly magazine on socially responsible
consumption.

Oxfam Trading
Murdoch Road, Bicester OX6 7RF
Supplies a variety of products from the Third World through
Oxfam shops or mail order catalogues.

Traidcraft PLC and Traidcraft Exchange
Kingsway, Gateshead NE11 0NE
Supplies a variety of goods from the Third World through mail
order, small shops and voluntary reps.

Third World Information Network and TWIN Trading
345 Goswell Road, London EC1V 7TJ
Support producers in the Third World and distribute fairly traded
products in the UK.

Traidéireann
PO Box 20, Athlone
Co Westmeath, Republic of Ireland
Supplies a variety of foods and crafts from the Third World.

World Development Movement
25 Beehive Place, London SW9 7QR
Campaigns on Third World issues, including fairer trade.